CHINESE MYTHOLOGY

CHINESE MYTHOLOGY

Anthony Christie

PAUL HAMLYN

UNIFORM WITH THIS EDITION:

Greek Mythology
Egyptian Mythology
North American Indian Mythology
Indian Mythology
Mexican and Central American Mythology
Oceanic Mythology
African Mythology
South American Mythology

The Hamlyn Publishing Group Limited
Hamlyn House
The Centre
Feltham
Middlesex

Contents

Colour Plates

Chronology of mythical and historical dynasties

THE THREE SOVEREIGNS
    Fu-hsi (also Fu-Hsi/Nu-kua as divine couple)
    Shen-nung
    Yen Ti
THE FIVE EMPERORS
    Huang Ti (Yellow Emperor)
    Chuan Hsiun
    Khun
    Yao
    Shun

Year	
C. 2000-1520 B.C.	HSIA DYNASTY (Yu, the founder, to Chieh)
C. 1520-1030 B.C.	SHANG (YIN) DYNASTY (Thang to Chou Hsin)
1030-221 B.C.	CHOU DYNASTY (Wu, first emperor)
C. 1030-722 B.C.	Early Chou Period
722-480 B.C.	Chhun Chhiu Period
480-221 B.C.	Warring States
221-207 B.C.	CHHIN DYNASTY (Shih Huang Ti, first unifier of China)
202 B.C.-A.D. 220	HAN DYNASTY
202 B.C.-A.D. 9	Earlier Han
A.D. 9-A.D. 23	Interregnum
A.D. 25-A.D. 220	Later Han
A.D. 221-265	SAN KUO PERIOD
	Shu Han
	Wei
	Wu
A.D. 265-420	CHIN DYNASTY
A.D. 420-479	SUNG DYNASTY
A.D. 479-581	(SIX DYNASTIES)
A.D. 581-618	SUI DYNASTY
A.D. 618-906	THANG DYNASTY
A.D. 907-960	(FIVE DYNASTIES)
A.D. 960-1126	NORTHERN SUNG DYNASTY
A.D. 1127-1279	SOUTHERN SUNG DYNASTY
A.D. 1260-1368	YUAN (Mongol) DYNASTY
A.D. 1368-1644	MING DYNASTY
A.D. 1644-1911	CHHING (Manchu) DYNASTY
A.D. 1912	REPUBLIC

The Chinese setting

It is hard to grasp the physical extent of the country which we know as China, whose more than three thousand years of written history provide a cultural continuity without parallel. In size China is continental: its area is about the same as Europe's. Its climates range from that of the sub-Arctic taiga of Manchuria to that of the sub-tropical jungles of the south-west. Its terrain is of great diversity: the upland plateau of Tibet, where the high ranges are covered with perpetual snow; the deserts and steppe of Central Asia; the rich deltas of the south-east coast, the great plains of the lower Yellow River valley.

Within this enormous space there is room for a great diversity of peoples and cultures. Nevertheless it is possible to discern a main group which dominates the entire area: it is this group that we call Chinese, and whose culture we have in mind when we talk of China. The various other ethnic groups within the political frontiers of China are almost all mongoloid peoples, as are the Chinese themselves; all have been influenced to a greater or a lesser extent, over the centuries, by the Chinese. But influences have not all flowed in one direction and, historically, what we call Chinese culture is itself the result of millenia of cross-fertilisation among numbers of different groups.

The point in time at which it is possible to identify a given group or aggregation of groups as being the Chinese (in anything approaching the modern sense) is difficult to determine, but it is perhaps reasonable to do so at the moment when the Chhin dynasty (249-207 B.C.) brought about the first unification of China. Though this did not last, Chhin Shih Huang Ti (221-210 B.C.) is thought of as the first Emperor. Under his successors of the Western and Eastern Han dynasties (206 B.C.-A.D. 220) a central government which ruled the whole country became a fact. This government, with minor interruptions, has persisted until the present day. The Chhin achievement has not been forgotten, however, and it is from this dynasty that the name China is derived – though the Chinese themselves have always preferred to refer to their country as the Middle Kingdom, *Chhung kuo.* When, about the beginning of the Christian era, news reached the Chinese of a great empire to the west of them – it was in fact that of Imperial Rome – they called it Ta Chhin after the first great empire in China itself. But although the Han dynasty made China a

A *thao-thieh* of the Shang or Yin period. This horned dragon or tiger monster lost its body as a punishment for eating human beings and was known as 'the glutton'. Its head or mask appears repeatedly in various stylised forms in the early artefacts. The eyebrows are *kuei* dragons. Museum of Far Eastern Antiquities, Stockholm.

reality, not all the regions inside today's political frontiers were included in the Han empire, and the country did not achieve its final extent until some centuries later.

Within the geographical space which we now call China there are three well marked zones. Of these the central one lies about the Yellow River, its main feature. There is every reason to believe that this region was the cradle of the nucleic culture, the core of Chinese civilisation. The zone to the north is that of the great plains of Manchuria, together with the Manchurian uplands and the mountainous regions drained by the Amur river. The mountains are forested, the plains now heavily eroded but once covered with mixed forest. The climate is continental and shows extreme variations. To the south of the Yellow River lies the third zone, which includes the area to the north of the Yangtze up to about the 33rd parallel, the Yangtze valley itself and the region to the south with its many rivers and lakes. Its western boundary is marked by the Tsinling mountains. Most of this region consists of hills, but there are two other well defined areas: the Szechwan basin, which is drained by the upper Yangtze; and the plain, towards the coast, which is drained by the lower Yangtze and the Huai river, itself a tributary of the Yangtze. Unlike the other two zones, this southern region has ample rainfall, with large areas of sub-tropical and tropical forest. The main crop is rice, whereas in the north the staples are wheat, millet, beans and kaoliang (sorghum). The central region, the Chinese homeland, has a temperate climate, with an adequate rainfall. Its western area consists of a loessic highland zone, from which there is a gradual transition to the rich alluvial plains to the east, while the Shantung peninsula forms a third sub-division. The mixed forest cover has been much reduced by human intervention and there is a general trend to semi-aridity.

Bronze pole end showing on one side a fierce human face surmounted by the symbol of drought, the destructive rain dragon known as the *thao-thieh*; and on the other side a deer and an elephant, creatures which in prehistoric times inhabited northern China. Such a ritual object would be significant both to hunters and to farmers. British Museum.

The early peoples

Ritual vessel for holding wine, of the type called *hu*. The decoration, of hunting scenes, shows bows and arrows and axes being wielded against buffalo and birds. The mainstay of the early Yellow River peoples, hunting remained important in the historical period. Huai river style, late Chou or Chhin dynasty, sixth to third century B.C. Minneapolis Institute of Arts.

Towards the end of the Pleistocene and at the beginning of the Holocene, the climate of northern China was much milder than at present. There was also a higher rainfall, so that many of the depressions ('nors') of Manchuria and the western edges of the central region were water-filled. Various animal species characteristic of a warm climate were found there, as was rice and bamboo, both now characteristic of the southern zone. Bamboo rat, elephant, rhinoceros, tapir and water buffalo all inhabited the north, as well as a number of warm water varieties of shellfish.

Yangshao

It was in such circumstances, in a setting very different from that to be found today, that hunter-fisher communities developed in the Yellow River drainage area. From these, neolithic groups emerged who were in turn to develop a culture which gave rise to the first historical cultures of China. These post-glacial developments in the north are culturally quite distinct from those to be found to the south of the Huai valley. There, cultural affinities were with South East Asia and not with the broad Eurasiatic tradition, linked with the woodland mesolithic cultures. But the developments in the south were the prototypes for the typical cultures of southern China in regions into which the people from the Yellow River were gradually to expand – a process which did not finish until the beginning of the Christian era, if indeed, it has ever wholly finished, since the movement south has never really come to a halt. But it is in the north, in the Yellow River valley, that the main interest lies, among the many thousands of neolithic sites.

From the hunter-fisher groups of the mesolithic period small village farming communities emerged in the region where the three modern provinces of Honan, Shansi and Shensi meet. Here, in the confluence area of three great

U. S. S. R.

Amur R

M O N G O L I A

NGKIANG-UIGHUR
(autonomous region)

M A N C H U R I A

I N N E R   M O N G O L I A

GREAT WALL

PEKING
(municipality)

NORTH
KOREA

K A N S S U

HOPEI

Pohai Bay

SOUTH
KOREA

H I N G H A I

NINGSIA-HUI
(autonomous
region)

Huan R

Fenhu R

S H A N S I

An-yang

Yellow R

SHANGTUNG

Y E L L O W

S E A

Weishui R

MT. TSINLING

Loyang

Cheng-chou

HONAN

T I B E T
(autonomous region)

Chialiang R

HUPEI

Yangtze R

KIANGSU

ANHWEI

SHANGHAI
(municipality)

NDIA

S Z E C H W A N

CHEKIANG

E A S T

B U R M A

KWEICHOW

HUNAN

KIANGSI-CHUANG
(autonomous region)

FUKIEN

C H I N A

S E A

YUNNAN

L A O S

KWANGSI

KWANTUNG

TAIWAN
(FORMOSA)

NORTH

VIETNAM

Hai Nan Tao

S O U T H   C H I N A   S E A

THAILAND

Philippine Islands

rivers, the Huangho, the Fenho and the Weishui, between the highland wooded zone and the swampy land to the east, food production appears to have reached a point at which it made possible mixed economy communities of agriculturalists, herdsmen and fishers, which gave rise in turn to the first historical cultures. During this crucial phase various culture traits developed: rice and millet were grown; pigs, cattle, sheep, dogs and poultry were domesticated (and the horse may have been); stamped earth houses with plastered floors and walls were constructed; silkworms were bred; cloth was woven from both silk and hemp and the first tailored clothes were probably produced. (To the south of China tailored garments were unknown, the characteristic garment being a wrap-round cloth of the sarong type.) Pottery of considerable sophistication was produced, including three-legged vessels

and steamers, and ceremonial vessels, together with jade artefacts, which seem to imply complex ritual occasions. There was a system of oracular prediction based upon the use of the shoulder-blades of animals.

The first stages of these developments took place during what is known as the Yangshao phase of Chinese prehistory and was concentrated around the junction of the three rivers. During the later parts of this phase the village groups gradually spread to other parts of the Yellow River valley, but the great expansion period did not occur until the so-called Lungshan phase, when the early farming culture suddenly expanded into the lower lying regions to the east and south.

Lungshan

It was long thought that the Lungshan and Yangshao cultures were quite distinct, but research during and after the war has shown that the Lungshan phase developed from Yangshao and was itself the precursor and foundation for the Yin-Shang culture, which is the first historical stage in the Chinese archaeological record. The great increase in food production and the expansion of farming communities during the Lungshan period saw the spreading of the culture through the entire area of the middle and lower Yellow River valley, the northern coastal region of Pohai Bay, the whole middle and lower Yangtze valley and much of the coast of Fukien and Kwangtung. Influences reached the hunter-fisher communities around the Lungshan periphery and it was during this phase that China may be said to have become a country of farmers. Within the Lungshan zone there was naturally room for regional variations, but there is no doubt that we are dealing with a single phenomenon which marks a further development from the Yangshao phase.

Permanent settlement became the normal rule, in place of Yangshao shifting settlements with repeated re-occupation of sites. Slash-and-burn cultivation gave way to more settled methods of agriculture which must surely have

A bronze *tsun*, ritual vessel for holding wine, in the shape of two rams with a *thao-thieh* mask between them. A variety of animals were domesticated and became familiar motifs as early as the Lungshan period. Shang dynasty, twelfth to eleventh century B.C. British Museum.

A bronze cheekpiece in the shape of a tiger's head. Hanging from a helmet, it was used to protect the face of the wearer in battle. Chan dynasty. British Museum.

A *kuang*, or vessel in which ceremonial millet wine was mixed, showing the fine detail achieved in bronze metallurgy by the Shang. The decorative motifs of the vessel itself are *thao-thieh* masks, while the lid is modelled as a tiger's or dragon's head with a serpent's tail curling behind. The handle consists of another mythical animal. Minneapolis Institute of Arts.

required fertilisers and irrigation. There was a rapid expansion of the settled zone and considerable regional variation within the single culture. Technical changes in tool forms and types can be detected, and wheel-made pottery began. There is also evidence for other types of specialised occupations. Divination by shoulder-blade was practised. Fortifications and weapons point to inter-village warfare. Evidence from burials seems to indicate the emergence of social distinctions within the group, whereas only age and sex seem to be differentiated in Yangshao burials. Finds of distinctive objects in restricted areas within a site seem to confirm the evidence for increasing social differentiation.

Ceremonial as opposed to domestic ceramic wares, including very fine eggshell vessels, are found, and there is some evidence for the existence of art not directly concerned with domestic objects, though it is insufficient to support the claim that its intention was religious or theocratic. Finally there is evidence that what appears to have been a simple fertility cult in the Yangshao phase gave place to an institutionalised ancestor cult and that ceremonials of much wider than agricultural intention were developed, possibly in association with specialised groups. Many of the elements of historical 'Chinese' culture can already be detected in the evidence of the Lungshan period.

The Lungshan communities depended upon agriculture. It seems that millet remained a staple; but in addition wheat and rice have been detected at sites as far north as Honan and Shensi. It is possible that rice was brought back from the south after the period of Lungshan expansion south of the Yangtze. Other crops definitely grown were varieties of peach, peanut, melon and waterchestnut, while sesame and beans were perhaps cultivated. The principal domestic animals remained the pig and the dog, but there is evidence for increasing numbers of cattle and sheep and, less certainly, for domesticated horses. Poultry was increasingly important. Amongst game, horse, boar, water deer, hare and bamboo rat have been identified, and there is clear evidence for large scale fishing. The shoulder-blades used for scapulimancy were of cattle and deer, with occasional sheep.

To the south-west of the Lungshan region, in the present day provinces of Szechwan, Yunnan, Kwangsi, Kweichou and western Kwangtung, there is evidence for neolithic settlements with

Goblet in the shape known as *ku*, from which wine was drunk in the sophisticated rituals elaborated by the Shang, and which were included in burials in order to nourish the soul. The decoration of the upper part takes the form of a *ko* dagger, a neolithic weapon associated with human sacrifice. Shang or Early Chou. Minneapolis Institute of Arts.

limited agriculture but still largely dependent upon fishing and the gathering of molluscs. It seems most likely that agriculture was introduced from Lungshan contacts, probably by way of the upper Yangtze and the Chialiang river. The farming of terraced fields, now so striking a feature of the Canton river valley and parts of highland Luzon, in the Philippines, is attested from the area of Ta-li in Yunnan, where natural creeks seem to have been used as the source of irrigation. If agriculture was introduced from the north, then it seems likely also that the cultivation of rice, the characteristic staple of China south of the Yangtze, was in fact a northern development – even though the plant itself, *oryza sativa*, originated in southern China or South East Asia.

Pole end in the form of a horned dragon. The use of mythological symbols to adorn domestic articles and chariot trappings followed an elaborate code established in Shang times. Bronze, Middle Chou dynasty (900-600 B.C.). Nelson Gallery, Kansas City.

The first historical period

Two tomb guards from a grave at Chinan in the Huai valley, Honan. While human sacrifices were carried out to provide the Shang rulers at Hsiao-thun with guards and servants, lesser burials and those of later times were more likely to be provided with such figurines. National Gallery, Prague.

Chinese historical tradition knows nothing of prehistory in the archaeologist's sense, but maintains that the cultural developments which prehistorians attribute to mesolithic and neolithic peoples were the work of the Three Sovereigns *San Huang* and the Five Emperors *Wu Ti*. These culture heroes were followed by three dynasties known as Hsia, Shang and Chou.

There was never any doubt about the existence of the Chou dynasty, but until relatively recently it was thought that the Hsia and Shang were as legendary as their imperial precursors. However, excavations at An-yang in Honan between 1927 and 1938 established the existence of the Shang dynasty and fully substantiated the account of it that was given in the *Shih Chi*, the history of China written by Ssu-ma Chhien in the first century B.C. So far, no trace has been found of the Hsia, but there still remains the possibility that it too will be confirmed by archaeological research. As we shall see, the area under Shang rule was limited and it is possible that Hsia and Shang were, in part at least, contemporary cultures.

The Shang

All the evidence indicates that the Shang emerged directly from the Lungshan phase in the areas where it has been established. The principal examples are in Honan where there is an uninterrupted and stratified succession of Yangshao, Lungshan, Shang. Although the chronology of the Shang is still uncertain, there is little reason to doubt the tradition that the dynasty was founded in 1766 B.C. (by Thang), that the capital was moved to An-yang in 1384 B.C. and that the dynasty was overthrown by Chou sometime between 1111 and 1027 B.C. Equally it seems clear that Shang can be seen as an evolution from the Lungshan phase, even if some elements in its cultural corpus cannot at present be derived from Lungshan prototypes. It seems likely that the fortified villages which, as we have already mentioned, are a feature of the Lungshan culture, developed into small states based upon a dominant village. As a result of warfare between such states one emerged as a major force, and it was this state which became Shang.

Certain new elements appeared in this period, three of which seem to distinguish Shang from its neolithic forerunners. These are the use of writing, bronze metallurgy and the horse chariot. Nothing is yet known of writing before the An-yang period of the Shang dynasty which, as we have just seen, falls well into the second part of the 650 or 750 years assigned to the dynasty. But the examples of writing from An-yang, almost entirely confined to the oracle bones, include characters which in style seem archaic and whose use seems to be ritual. This furnishes some evidence for an earlier stage of writing which need not, however, predate the Shang dynasty. There is clear evidence for bronze objects before An-yang, notably from Cheng-chou, where the items are fewer in number and less advanced than at An-yang itself. But there is as yet no evidence that metallurgy reached China from the west, though the use of bronze seems very much earlier in the Middle East. Technically and technologically Chinese bronze metallurgy exhibits a number of features which distinguish it from other early bronze-using systems. It may well be that, even if the idea of metallurgy reached China from elsewhere, its actual development was native, and that this too is to be seen as a Shang development. The existence of the horse chariot at Shang sites is at present without any previous history; horse bones are, however, recorded at Lungshan sites, though unfortunately there is nothing to show whether the animals were eaten or ridden.

The area for which true Shang sites can be established lies in northern and western Honan, southern Hopei and

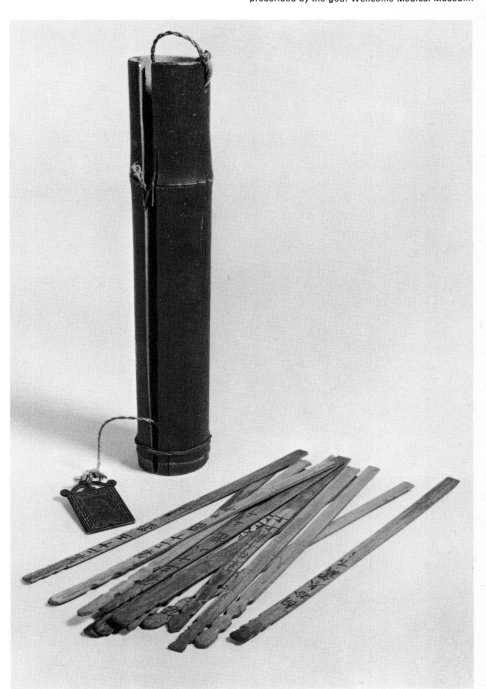

The oracular consultation of the gods begun in the Shang period changed little in essence in later times. This *tsien tung* cylinder was used by patients presenting themselves at the shrine of the god of medicine. It was shaken until one of the sticks fell out; the inscription on the stick indicated the cure prescribed by the god. Wellcome Medical Museum.

Hou Chi, a miraculously born descendant of Huang Ti. As one of the gods of the earth, he was made Ruler of the Millet by Thang, founder of the Shang dynasty. When the Shang were supplanted by the Chou, Hou Chi was called ancestor of the Chou. Statuette in bronze. Musée Guimet.

western Shantung. It is probable that south-east Honan was also part of Shang's domain; other sites in Shensi, Shansi and Anhwei may also have belonged to the central Shang tradition. Material with some Shang elements from Szechwan and Kiangsi should not be attributed to Shang but rather explained as being influenced by Shang.

A characteristic Shang centre exhibits certain quite distinctive features which form a pattern. There is a cluster of villages forming a settlement group, with some evidence for specialisation between the villages (an extension perhaps of the specialist quarters within a village already detectable at later Lungshan sites). An aristocratic complex can be recognised within the settlement group. It is distinguished by the presence of ceremonial altars, rectangular houses with stamped earth floors, pillar foundations in stone (sometimes stone figures to serve as pillar supports), and complex grave systems. These include enormous tombs with human and animal sacrifices and the burial of horse chariots. There is evidence, in the form of oracle bones and complex sacrifices with ceremonial pottery and bronze objects, of sophisticated rituals and ceremonials. Status is strongly marked by the difference in horse trappings, chariot fittings and various grades of artefacts, pottery, ornaments and bronze utensils. Cowries may have been used as currency. Certain types of pottery and of forms of bronze vessel, quite distinct from earlier stone and ceramic forms, are also distinctive of Shang sites; so are the very large numbers of stone sickles, greatly in excess of those found in Lungshan contexts. The use of elaborately prepared bones for scapulimancy and the introduction of turtle shell for oracular purposes is also characteristic.

From the archaeological evidence at An-yang itself and the great site at Cheng-chou it is possible to infer a considerable amount about the nature of the Shang state. These inferences can be supplemented by information gleaned from the oracle bones and from traditional Chinese historical sources. Inevitably there are large gaps and some of the conclusions so far arrived at must be treated with caution, but the picture that emerges is reasonably clear.

THE SHANG CITY

The Shang city had a central area enclosed within one or more walls where the state temples and the palace, as well as the homes of the state functionaries, probably members of the royal family in many cases, were located. These functionaries included priests whose role, in view of the central importance of the oracle system, must have been of the greatest significance in the administration. Outside the wall were the various specialist quarters of the city and the dwelling places of the people, both free and slave, including, so far as one can judge, numbers of agriculturalists working nearby fields.

There must have been a considerable population, though it is possible that labour from outside the immediate city area was also brought in. At Cheng-chou it has proved possible to make some calculations about the size of labour force required to construct the city wall. This was some 7,200 metres in length and enclosed an area of 3.2 sq. kilometres. The greatest surviving height of wall is just over 9 metres and it seems reasonable to suppose that originally a 10 metre wall existed. The actual base is 36 metres at its widest. The whole is of rammed earth, and it can be shown that its construction required something of the order of 2,900,000 cubic metres of soil. Experiments have shown that it is possible to move between 0.02 and 0.03 cubic metres of earth an hour using a bronze or a stone hoe. The Chinese archaeologist An Chin-huai has shown that on the basis of calculations such as these we may envisage a labour force of 10,000 men working for eighteen years to complete the great fortification which is the citadel of Cheng-chou – a task which implies a state with impressive resources and considerable administrative capacity to draw upon.

Outside the enclosure have been found two bronze foundries, a large workshop for the manufacture of bone tools and implements, a pottery-making area with no less than fourteen kilns and a possible vintner's establishment. Large numbers of storage pits were found and various types of burials. There is evidence for the formal interment of both dogs and cattle, which seems to imply some ritual significance, though it is not known what this was. Human burials at Cheng-chou were of two types: with grave goods and, though in two instances only, human sacrifices; and another series of much smaller graves, with very few or no grave furnishings.

The An-yang site still remains the most important source for information about the Shang, despite the interruption to the excavations following Japan's attack on China and the incomplete publication of the results obtained until then. It is clear that here we are dealing with a royal city. The site extends for some kilometres along either bank of the Huan river and consists of a number of apparently more or less self-sufficient settlements in close relation with one another and with an administrative centre, the royal enclave at Hsiao-thun, with which was also linked a royal cemetery at Hsi-pei-kang. The identi-

Solid bronze plaque depicting a leaping tiger. The incised decoration suggests wings; the tiger, which in the autumn descended from the mountains in the west, was mythologically associated with the autumn and the west and, though known to the Chinese, was often treated as a fabulous beast. Chou dynasty. British Museum.

fication of the latter depends upon the ostentation of the burials and to that extent is tentative, but it is difficult to see that such conspicuous consumption could have been linked with anything less than a royal house.

In the Hsiao-thun centre, which appears to have been divided into three sections, though these may represent subsequent building stages, many of the buildings are associated with burials, which were probably ritually significant. It seems likely that one section was a dwelling quarter, the second the temple area, and the third reserved for ritual and ceremonial purposes. Almost all the buildings have stamped earth platforms at their base, in marked contrast to the semi-underground dwellings in the rest of the An-yang site. Those identified as palaces or temples are accompanied by pit buildings which housed storage facilities, workshops (including foundries, potteries, bone

manufactories), and were also presumably the homes of servants and the slaves' quarters.

The storage pits at Hsiao-thun yielded more than 10,000 of the inscribed oracle bones whose method of use and function is discussed below. The building of each was accompanied by human sacrifices and the slaughter of dogs. The humans lay holding bronze vessels or faced outwards with halberds in their hands as ghostly wardens of the buildings which they surrounded. In the central court there were five burials of chariots, each with its charioteer. But the scale of sacrifice within the royal enclave is as nothing compared with that at the royal cemetery.

Eleven great graves were found there. It has been estimated that the moving of the earth alone would have required 7,000 man-days. They would correspond in number with the eleven rulers, from Phan-keng (who moved the capital to An-yang) to Ti-yih, whose successor the emperor Shun, the last ruler, is reported to have been burned to death when the Chou invaders overthrew the Shang capital. The tomb consists of a great central pit, about seven metres square, with walls sloping back to the surface. The body was placed in a large coffin of wood in the centre of the pit over a small hole containing a sacrificed dog. From the level of the top of the coffin ramps, fifteen to twenty metres long, led to the surface; on these, as on the berms of the pit in which the coffin was placed, were the bodies of slaughtered horses and men in their scores. Sometimes the human victims had been beheaded and their heads placed in separate heaps from their bodies. These may have been prisoners captured in battle.

SHANG RELIGIOUS BELIEFS

All these victims seem to have died to furnish the dead lord with his servitors in the next world. There he, in turn, would serve his descendants by advising them of the actions appropriate to the situations put to him on the oracle bones ever after.

The method of oracular communication used by the Shang was really quite

Dragon pendant in brown jade. The dragon symbolised the east, one of the deities to which the Shang made sacrifices. Jade ornaments were particularly prized, partly for their intrinsic beauty and partly because it was so difficult to work the hard material with the primitive tools of the Shang. This pendant dates from the later feudal period or Eastern Chou (772-221 B.C.). Seattle Art Museum.

simple and seems to have been developed during the Lungshan period. Then, the shoulder-blade of a cow was burnt with a hot point in order to produce cracks whose significance could be interpreted by an augurer. By the time of the An-yang site the process had been made more systematic. The question to be put was usually inscribed on the bone (where sometimes the answer was recorded too). A circular pit, which might be overlain by an oval one, was made in the bone and a heated bronze point was applied to the edge of the pit. The resultant cracks on the other side of the bone were then interpreted by the augurer as giving a favourable or unfavourable answer. The questions asked of the bone were usually about rain or crops, the prospects for hunting, the advisability of royal travel or of military campaigning, or making sacrifices to the ancestors.

It was these royal ancestors who were

divine (whether the living king was so considered is uncertain) who were responsible for communication between the living and the spirit world and whose benevolence ensured the prosperity of the state, a prefiguration of the later situation in which a dynasty reigned until Heaven withdrew its support. Because the names of the ancestors occur on the oracle bones, it has been possible to confirm the reliability of the Shang king list in the traditional histories. We can also show that there was originally a preference for fraternal succession which finally gave place to that from father to son.

But these ancestors were not the only spirits to whom official offerings were made. The supreme deity, Shang Ti or Ti, appears to have ruled in Heaven as the dynastic king ruled on earth and, in addition to controlling natural phenomena (which could markedly affect the prosperity of his worshippers),

Overleaf left. Li Thieh-kuai, one of the Eight Immortals of Taoism, who lived in the Yuan (Mongol) dynasty but was said to have received instruction from Lao Tzu himself. He had magical powers and the gourd he carried contained medicines which could revive the dead. Porcelain figure, c. nineteenth century. Wellcome Medical Museum.

Overleaf right. Shou-lao, the god of longevity, who was at first a stellar deity, the Old Man of the South Pole under whose influence the nation enjoyed peace. He is characterised by his large bald head and the peach, symbol of long life, which he carries. Wellcome Medical Museum.

The Red Bird or phoenix, which symbolised the south, a cardinal direction honoured by the Shang. The phoenix later became identified with the pheasant, but this bird, with its curved beak and long claws, is of the archaic type: a bird of prey more aptly associated with the arid south. Bas relief from the tomb of Shen in Szechwan. Han dynasty.

A *wu* shaman or exorcist. Shamanism, the earliest form of cult in China, and relying on magic, was intended to give men power over the gods. Its appeal was of longer duration and more popular than any of the philosophies, so that it gradually took over and transformed Taoism and Chinese Buddhism. Possibly from the Lo-yang district. *c.* third century A.D.

he seems to have been a god of agriculture. Shang Ti was assisted by various departmental deities, a pattern which was to persist in Chinese religion until modern times. Such deities did not receive sacrifices directly, but were approached through the ancestors. There was also a god of earth or of the soil, She or Thu (with, it seems likely, local soil deities in each centre), as well as gods of the directions and of the hills and rivers. Every single one of these deities was entitled to sacrifices and all might be approached with requests for rain in time of drought.

Sacrifices were made to an Eastern Mother and a Western Mother and to a Ruler of the Four Quarters. They were also made to east, west, and south – but never to north, and to the source of the Huan river (who once received an offering of four cattle), as well as to the God of the Yellow River. The cult of these deities was generally in the hands of *wu* shamans, and was accompanied by music and dancing. Instruments included drums and an object like an ocarina. There were also bells and stone or jade chimes.

Cheng Te-khum has described the religious beliefs of the Shang as being based on a philosophy that the universe was composed of three levels, the heavenly world above, the earthly world underneath and the human world in between. The religious practices were fundamentally human institutions and they were extended to entertain also the gods in Heaven and the deities of the Earth. This was probably the beginning of the Chinese philosophy that tried to unite the three spheres into one. The world of the supernatural, the world of nature and the world of man were beginning to be bound up in an all-embracing unity with man as its centre. In his lifetime the Shang Chinese might be associated with the other two worlds through offerings and sacrifices, but after death he continued to live and was free to enter the three spheres as he chose.

Thus the centre of the universe was man. The entire universe including the Heaven and the Earth existed for him. The supernatural as well as natural beings or powers were but tools of man and they could be persuaded to do anything for his welfare, either by offerings and sacrifices or through the personal persuasion of his ancestors. This is the pragmatic philosophy on which the Chinese way of life was founded and it has continued to be one of the strongest currents in the stream of Chinese civilisation and culture.

The growth of a feudal society

The rise of Chou

The Shang capital finally fell to the troops of Chou sometime between the end of the twelfth and the end of the eleventh century B.C. (1122-1027 B.C.). Chou was one of the feudatory states of Shang situated in the Weishui valley, Shensi, and there is little reason to believe that its culture differed essentially from that of Shang. This view, however, has only recently gained general support. It was not until the second part of the Chou period, known as Eastern Chou, after the capital had moved to Lo-yang (771 B.C.) that any really marked change in the pattern of Chinese culture can be detected. Sites which have been investigated in the Western (i.e. earlier) Chou area show a succession of Yang-shao, Lungshan, and Chou. It seems clear that originally Chou was little more than another manifestation of Lungshan post-neolithic evolution. What is not clear is whether the markedly Shang elements in Chou sites predate the fall of An-yang or not; but there are references in Shang oracle bones which make it clear that Chou was a force to be reckoned with. Indeed, there is some evidence in the bones to suggest that Shang provoked attacks by third parties upon Chou, and that the overthrow of the dynasty was the result of Chou counterattacks. Once Chou achieved power it exercised at least nominal rule over China for almost a thousand years.

Bronze tiger with a hollow chamber in the centre. Chou dynasty, c. tenth century B.C. Though the decorative motifs show the Chou development of Shang culture, the general style is quite different: more massive and in keeping with the power of the dynasty, which came from the west, the direction of the tiger. Freer Gallery, Washington, D.C.

Although at first Chou may have ruled directly the whole area that had been Shang and, indeed, even extended the area that fell within its suzerainty – there are records of Chou campaigns as far as the eastern seaboard – it was obviously impossible for later Chou rulers to exercise direct power over the whole domain. The practice therefore developed of stationing powerful garrisons, whose commanders were loyalists, in areas remote from the capital (which remained to the west of the region, at Tsung Chou, until 770 B.C.). Inevitably, however, such garrisons shifted in the course of time from military subordination to the ruler into a feudatory pattern of relationship in which the remoteness of the garrison or the extent of its power determined the degree to which its commander was controllable by the king. By the time the capital was moved to Lo-yang, twelve states had emerged whose loyalty to the centre was scarcely more than nominal, but whose rulers required the services of the king for various ritual purposes and as a source of honours and rewards. This common and necessary attachment to the centre did little or nothing to prevent more or less incessant warfare between the states.

CHOU BELIEFS

During the rule of the Chou dynasty the great rituals were developed which are described in such detail in the *Li Chi* and the *I Li*, the two compendious works which govern all aspects of right behaviour, whether public or private. There were no priests to conduct the rituals thus prescribed. For the household, its head was the proper functionary, for the state the king. *Li*, which we commonly translate as ritual, is best thought of as subsuming the concept of order and social harmony within a strictly hierarchical system. Heaven was in concord with society so long as society was harmonious: malfunctioning of the social order or malpractice by the ruler was met by disasters for which Heaven was responsible. Heaven, Thien, replaced Shang Ti as the supreme deity (if we may use the word about a non-anthropomorphised concept).

Some concept of personal religion seems to have existed – a man was thought to have two souls, only one of

Ceremonial jade sceptre used by the king in his all-important mediating role between the state and Heaven, Thien. As the king alone was capable of performing the ritual for the benefit of society, it is appropriate that the sceptre combines the circular *pi* symbol of Heaven and the axe symbol of royal power. Shang dynasty. National Gallery, Prague.

which survived him for any length of time – but for the most part the practice of religion seems to have been a matter for the lower orders and not for the ruling classes or the educated. The villagers supported the shaman and the witch doctor and made the offerings to the spirits of the countryside. The court was concerned only with those observances which kept Heaven and Earth in harmonious balance. There was none the less a place, particularly among the ruling houses, for the traditions of the hero-ancestors of each lineage. They continued to receive their due cult because they continued to mediate between Man and Heaven, and, it appears, because they provided, as they had done in Shang times, the evidence for the line's legitimate claim to exercise power in the land.

Thus, as groups on the periphery of the Chou state began to be incorporated into it, the rulers of such groups were in their turn endowed with a Chinese lineage. Of the powerful state of Chhu which by now lay well to the south of the original Chou area, we discover 'The princes of Chhu are the descendants of Chhung and Li' and we know that traditionally Chhung and Li are connected with Shao Hao, one of the legendary rulers before the time of Hsia and Shang (see also p. 60). The situation among those peripheral groups which did not willingly embrace Chinese culture and tradition is equally illuminating. The Chinese seem to have recognised that their social order was more or less as sophisticated as that of the Chinese themselves; they displayed *li*, but they were troublesome and often actively hostile, so their tribal name was often prefaced in Chinese with the pejorative *chhuan*, dog. But, as Karlgren has explained, in the belief of their Chinese contemporaries, their ruling houses must have derived from Chinese families, otherwise no social order could have been present: therefore 'their leaders were considered descendants of decadent members of Chinese grandee families'. For example, the *chhuan* Jung (a people living just to the west of Chou) were considered as descendants of

Two warriors. The Chou dynasty gradually crumbled during the period from 480 to 221 B.C. known as the Warring States. The art of war and of the deployment of armies was markedly developed during the long struggle. The symbolism of power was never far from mind, as the traditional accoutrement of these warriors shows. Taoist scroll painting.

Warfare led to the interpenetration of various local cultures and so built up the Chinese tradition. This plaque depicting a fabulous beast and a ram is in the 'Ordos' style borrowed from the tribes of Mongolia and Siberia, who loved to depict fierce animal conflicts reminiscent of their own attacks on the outlying provinces of China. By the Han period, such styles were entirely assimilated. Collection Franco Vannotti.

Detail from a Han pottery tile depicting the legendary meeting of Lao Tzu and Confucius. Confucius lived from 551 to 479 B.C. The actual existence of Lao Tzu is less certain, but his followers claimed that he lived around 590 B.C. Nevertheless his philosophy was, like Confucianism, a reaction to troubled times. Musée Cernuschi.

the mythical ruler Chuan Hu, but only through his ne'er-do-well son Thao Wu who was identified with a demon of the same name, a situation which, as Karlgren remarks, is 'a typical example of the workings of the archaic Chinese mind'.

The emergence of Chhin

The wars between the states inevitably weakened the country as a whole and the various non-Chinese tribes living to the west were not slow to take advantage of this. Northern Honan was devastated in 660 B.C. in the course of an invasion that may well have brought certain new art styles to China. The incorporation of Chhu into the Chinese state led to the rapid spread southwards of Chinese culture. There it found the people eager for the advanced technology of their northern neighbours. At the same time various ideas and stories belonging to the southern tribes found their way into the Chinese repertory.

Nevertheless, the ruler of Chhu was to arrogate to himself the title *wang*, king, in 704 B.C., though this was the prerogative of the ruler of Chou and two kings in a single feudatory system are impossible. The internecine warfare continued, and it is not without reason that the period 403-221 B.C., is known as 'The Warring States'.

During this period the state of Chhin, situated in the hills to the west, was most aggressive towards the states of the central area; ultimately it was the Chhin

ruler Shih Huang Ti who ruled over a unified China in 221 B.C. as the first historical emperor. It was he, incidentally, who was responsible for linking together the various small defences constructed by states along the western marches to form them into the Great Wall of China.

This feat of construction serves to illustrate a major development in Chinese society. The government had learned how to utilise to the full the comparatively large resources of manpower which were available, and public works on a great scale became a feature of the Chinese state. Thus a canal was dug to link the lower waters of the Yangtze and the Yellow River. In another sphere, the forces engaged in battle were no longer mere handfuls of skirmishers but ran into tens of thousands. This control over human resources seems to have been achieved by a high degree of control and manipulation of food supplies for the riverine populations and by assuring their safety through undertakings to minimise the constant risk of flooding; and such operations required works conducted on the large scale of state rather than local construction work.

During this period certain philosophies began to emerge which were profoundly to affect the future. It is interesting to speculate on the extent to which they were the response to an interest in and concern with effective government. For whatever one may think of the works of Confucius and

Mencius, they were both the advocates of a philosophy for the ruling class while preaching that cosmic order depended upon submission to the existing order and hierarchy. There were two other systems current: that of Motzu who preached that family affection should be extended to embrace all mankind (an idea which was certainly anathema to Confucius and his followers); and that attributed to Lao Tzu which advocated a submission to the Tao and of which it has been said that its 'quietist and anti-rational tenor... has attracted an interest in the West in recent times almost comparable to that which Confucian concepts held for the French *philosophes* of the eighteenth century!'

The unification of China

The year 221 B.C. was a turning point in Chinese history since it marked, in the words of a Chinese scholar, 'the consolidation of the Chinese as a single people with a single culture and a sense of common nationality'. Though not everyone would be quite so absolute as this, it is true that, after a number of years during which the various warring states were pacified – Chou itself in 256 B.C. and the Shantung state of Chhi in 221 – China (or rather its north and central parts) was unified under a single dynasty. The situation did not last, but under the Han the whole of what we now call China was brought under the central government. Han remains are found in every province of China and in many parts of Manchuria; Han sites occur in considerable numbers everywhere, clear proof that Han culture was general; finally all the remains found belong to a single cultural tradition which we can safely call Chinese.

What had happened was that the gradual process of cultural unification had now been followed by a political one. And although in peripheral areas, particularly in the south-west and, to a lesser extent, in the coastal region to the south of the Yangtze delta, strong local elements persisted, the reality of central government and political control was a potent factor in the accelerated process of assimilation and conformity to the Han pattern. It was during the period from the accession of Shih Huang Ti to the end of the later Han dynasty that the nucleic culture of the Yellow River, augmented by accessions from the regions which had gradually come under its influence, spread southward beyond the valley of the Yangtze to the present borders of Indochina. During this process, as the Chinese penetrated the various cultural zones to the south, many new elements entered the corpus of Chinese tradition and belief.

It is against the background of this long history of the emergence of China and of the slow process of southward expansion and absorption that we must view the mythology and legends of China and the Chinese.

The sorceress Hsi Wang Mu shown on this Han or Six Dynasties bronze mirror with her consort Tung Wang Kung. She is represented as the Queen of the West in her early form when she inhabited a Jade mountain beyond Khun-lun and was the tiger-toothed mistress of plague and disaster. They are accompanied by spirit figures mounted on winged horses and deer. Seattle Art Museum.

Tiger leaping down a hill. Tigers were honoured as the emblems of the west, the direction of Khun-lun and the Western Paradise; but they were also feared, for if one ate a man his soul became the tiger's slave and preyed upon other men. Painting by Chen Chu-chung. British Museum.

Bronze horse of the Thang dynasty. Horses were popular subjects under the military rulers from the Han to the Mongols, but they had earlier mythological significance too. Khun appeared as a white horse; a dragon-horse brought the *pa kua* to Fu-hsi; and as protectors against demons, horses were placed on guard outside tombs. Tenth century A.D. British Museum.

The ox was originally a star-deity, but through his own stupidity he was forced to remain on earth to help farmers with their ploughing. He bore men no grudge, however. Many, such as the father of the Thai girl and his companions, were regarded as holy animals, especially under Indian influence. Seventeenth-century jade. Ming dynasty. Victoria and Albert Museum.

The myths and their sources

A fundamental problem confronts every student of Chinese mythology. We are lucky that we possess a vast body of Chinese literature and historical material, a corpus of written sources more ancient and continuous than for any other people. But although much of it purports to belong to the period of Shang and Chou – the archaeological record of which we have already considered – this is not actually the case. Texts abound, and all have their commentaries and comments upon the commentators. But the greater part of these are compilations of a much later date than appears at first sight, generally Han. And such compilations are usually the work of scholars who used supposedly old and traditional material to sustain their own viewpoints by giving them an air of legitimacy.

Li Szu and the burning of books

A number of the best known Chinese philosophers lived in the period of the Warring States when, we may assume, some of the feudal traditions and practices were still living. But already Chinese society was in a state of flux and one has the impression that such scholars as Confucius were attempting to restore an imaginary status quo in reaction to the social changes amidst which they were living and which they deplored. Some evidence in support of this view can be found in Ssu-ma Chhien's account of a proposal made in 213 B.C. by Li Szu, minister of Shih Huang Ti. Li Szu is execrated among scholars for his proposal, which the emperor accepted, for the burning of all books, save technical manuals and handbooks; and it is partly as a result of his action that we are so inadequately furnished with early Chinese myths and legends. His proposal is of value, however, in setting out clearly the attitude of the scholar class and serves

to explain, in our present context, some of the reasons why post-Chhin texts must be viewed with scepticism as original source material. For what was reconstructed tended to reflect a highly selective version of tradition, favourable largely to the *chuntzu* scholar class. Li Szu's memorial went as follows:

The Five Emperors did not copy each other, the Three Dynasties did not imitate their predecessors. Each had its own particular form of government. It was not that they were opposed to the methods of their predecessors but that times had changed. Now Your Majesty has brought about a great achievement, and founded a glory that will last for ten thousand years. But narrow-minded scholars cannot understand this. The proposals of Shun-yu are based upon practices in the Three Dynasties, but why should we take them as a model? [Shun-yu, a conservative minister, had argued in favour of re-establishing a system of fiefs, on the grounds that they had always existed.] The princes used always to be at war. They paid much attention to itinerant scholars and relied on their advice. But now the realm has been pacified and law and order emanates from a single authority. The common people are engaged upon industry and agriculture while the superior people study law and administration. Only the scholars fail to conform to the new trends and study the past in order to deprecate the present. They cause doubts and misgivings among the black-haired [the people – the usual phrase for the peasantry]. The Counsellor, your servant Li Szu, aware that in offering incorrect advice he may incur the death penalty, proposes as follows:

In the past the realm was divided and troubled: none could unite it,

Confucius, whose works upholding the aristocratic order to which he belonged were reinterpreted under the Han to support the ruling Son of Heaven and to justify the power of the current dynasty in terms of tradition. The scholar class itself stood to benefit from the resurgence of the great philosopher. Statuette showing him dressed as a mandarin. Late Ming/early Chhing. Musée Guimet.

Kuan Yu, one of the generals in the period known as the Three Kingdoms, which in the second century A.D. brought the Han dynasty to an end in a period of disorder similar to that which ushered it in. In these times hereditary generals flourished. Thus Kuan Yu was later deified as Kuan Ti, god of war. Rubbing from stone engraving. British Museum.

Scholars studying the symbols of the *yin* and *yang* principles, the cardinal principles of the universe which philosophers tried to bring into harmony and which were basic to so much Chinese mystical symbolism. Their effort to seek out first causes made the scholars seem obscurantist troublemakers to Li Szu. Seventeenth century. British Museum.

Right. Fu-hsi, first of the Three Sovereigns and supposed inventor of the *pa kua*, the eight trigrams, which lie on the ground before him. In addition to their role in divination the *pa kua* were the basis of Chinese calligraphy, so scholars especially revered Fu-hsi who, despite his 'archaic' dress, is seen with the long nails worn by scholars. The tortoise before him is a reminder that tortoise shells were used as oracle bones. Portrait by Ma Lin. Sung dynasty. National Museum of Taiwan.

Many princes ruled at the same time. Scholars rely in their discussions upon the old times in order to decry the present and use false instances to create confusion in current matters. They proclaim the excellence of what they have studied in order to denigrate the achievements of Your Majesty. Now that the whole realm is in the hands of a single ruler, they praise the past and keep themselves aloof. When they hear of a new edict, they criticise it in the light of their researches for they oppose new laws and orders. At Court they are discreet, but elsewhere they indulge in public debate and encourge the common people to believe their calumnies. This being so, if no action is taken, the imperial authority will be diminished, and the power of the dissident will increase. This must be prevented. Your servant proposes that the Histories, save that of Chhin, shall be burnt. Except for those of the rank of Scholar of Great Learning [of whom there were only seventy] everyone throughout the realm who possesses a copy of the *Shu Ching*, the *Shih Ching* and the works of the Hundred Schools [of philosophy] must take them to the magistrates to be burnt. Those who dare to discuss or comment upon the *Shu Ching* and the *Shih Ching* shall be put to death and their bodies exposed in the market place. Those who laud ancient institutions to the disparagement of the present regime shall be exterminated with their families. Officials who condone breaches of this order shall be treated as accomplices. Anyone who has not burnt his books within thirty days of this order shall be branded and sent to forced labour at the Great Wall. Only those books which treat of medicine, divination, agriculture and arboriculture shall be allowed. Those who wish to study law and administration may do so by modelling themselves upon officials of the government. There is no doubt of the reality of the destruction, as the deaths of 460 scholars on charges of concealing books testifies.

Taoist priest's robe of brocade embroidered with the eight trigrams, which were linked with the five elements, earth, metal, water, wood, fire and, in the centre, the interlocked symbols of *yin* and *yang*. *Yin* and *yang* and their manifestation in the elements were thought from late Chou times to constitute the Tao or Way, the principle of the universe, and were the basis of court ritual. Eighteenth to nineteenth centuries. Metropolitan Museum of Art, New York.

That so much survived is a tribute to the scholars who were the object of Li Szu's attack; that so much of what survives belongs to the Confucian school demonstrates how widely that particular school of philosophy had spread. The decree none the less broke the continuity of tradition and it is clear, for example from the work of Ssu-ma Chhien, that much difficulty was experienced in understanding parts of the ancient literature which had been laboriously reconstructed under the Han. Ssu-ma Chhien appears to have totally failed to understand the distinction, critically important for a grasp of the power structure in feudal China, between clan and family names. As has been remarked by a western scholar of the period: 'So completely had the aristocracy lost caste and position at the end of the revolution that a scholar and a conservative no longer clearly understood that their ancient privileges had been founded on noble descent and not on education.'

The fall of Chhin

Although the decree ended the hope of those who wished to restore the feudal system, it also brought about the end of Chhin: nobility, scholars and peasants alike united in their hatred of the Chhin military overlords whose oppression seemed far more onerous than that of the feudal lords of the past. As a Han scholar wrote:

> From princes and ministers to the humblest of the people all were terrified and went in fear of their lives. No man was secure in office: all were liable to degradation. Thus Chhen She [a commoner and soldier from Chhu who initiated the first mutiny against Shih Huang Ti's successor] without needing to be a sage like Thang or Wu [who founded the Shang and Chou dynasties], without having any high rank . . . had only to wave his arms for the whole realm to answer like an echo. When a man has the rank of Son of Heaven and all the wealth of the realm as his resources and yet cannot escape slaughter it is because he has failed to distinguish between the means by

which power is maintained safely and the causes of disaster.

The revolt which Chhen She initiated was suppressed, but many further rebellions followed and it is interesting to note that each of the groups tended to set up its independent king in the old tradition, their candidates being obscure members of the old royal families. Ultimately two leaders emerged, Liu Pang a commoner and future founder of the Han dynasty, and Hsiang Yu, a Chhu aristocrat who was also a hereditary general.

At first the aristocrat appeared to emerge successful. He set up a state in which territories were distributed to various of his supporters and to Chhin generals who had changed sides. Liu Pang was granted a realm in Szechwan and parts of Shensi, known as Han from the local river. The feudal system which Hsiang Yu tried to re-establish proved quite unequal to the problems of the new state in which he ruled as Pa Wang or supreme king. Bloody fighting broke out between the various holders of land, but in the end this resolved itself into a struggle between Liu Pang and Hsiang Yu. The war lasted five years and ended in victory for Liu Pang, who established his capital in Shensi.

Liu Pang gave fiefs to his followers but reserved the title of king for members of his own family, none the less appointing imperial officers to oversee their rule. His victorious generals were gradually deprived of the lands which they had received as reward for their support and most were degraded in rank: many were put to death. One of Liu Pang's successors had the ingenious idea of making all the sons of a feudal lord his coheirs. As a result the number of fiefs increased, since the lands held had to be fragmented to meet the demands of the heirs, but each fief became less and less significant with every succeeding generation.

Finally, Liu Pang and his successors employed the strongest advocates of theoretical feudalism, the old scholar class, to justify the idea that all were subservient to the state in the person of the ruler.

Shang or early Chou wine vessel in the shape of an owl. Owls seem to have been of mythological significance from the earliest times. As nocturnal creatures they represented the dark, negative *yin* elements of the universe, and may well have represented Chaos, *hun-tun*, which had to be destroyed to bring order into the world. Minneapolis Institute of Arts.

Right. The Seven Sages of the Bamboo Grove, a group of Taoist scholars living in the late third century A.D. who, rejecting Confucian orthodoxy and equally the magical practices of the *wu* shamans, developed Chuang-tzu's philosophy of non-action. They were ridiculed as eccentric drunkards and persecuted for their unwillingness to bend philosophy to support the changing dynasties. Silk tapestry of the late eighteenth century. Lyons Museum.

Confucianism rewritten

The books which had been destroyed under Shih Huang Ti were now reconstructed but re-interpreted to provide a picture of the past in which the feudal period was seen as a degenerate phase in a once unified empire which the Han dynasty had now restored. The works of Confucius which had been devised as a codification of aristocratic ethics were now extended to furnish a universal system. The interpretation and maintenance of this system was to be the function of the scholar class, whose status depended upon education and not, as in the time of Confucius, upon birth.

The decree promoted by Li Szu was repealed in 191 B.C. though it had not been enforced since the fall of the Chhin dynasty. Han scholars set about the reconstruction of the texts which had been destroyed, and since they were mainly followers of Confucius it was the works of that sage and those who were considered as of his school which received the main attention. These books are what are usually referred to as the Classics. Among the most important is the *Shu Ching*, the Book of History. Of this there are two texts: one, the so-called 'old' text, was alleged to have been found hidden in the wall of Confucius' own house and edited by one of his descendants, Khung An-kuo. The other, the 'modern' text (the epithet refers to the new style of calligraphy in which it was written), was preserved by Fu Sheng, who had been a member of the Academy set up under Li Szu's decree and was said to have written down twenty-nine chapters by heart. (In another version he too had hidden his text in the wall of his house during the persecutions under Shih Huang Ti.) The *Shu Ching* consists of documents, speeches, proclamations and orations belonging to various historical or pseudo-historical events. Another work is the *Shih Ching* or Book of Songs, an anthology of ancient poems which caused much trouble to Confucian scholars since their subjects, often frank accounts of sexual licence and desire, had to be interpreted in political and ethical terms. The *I*

Part of the celebrated Nine Dragon scroll, painted in 1244 by the Taoist poet and painter Chhen Jung, which shows the manifestation of dragons from the ocean waves and from the clouds. Besides being the auspicious bringers of rain and the symbol of the emperor, dragons, according to the Taoists, were symbolic of the Way, the central truth of their philosophy, which revealed itself momentarily only to vanish in mystery. Museum of Fine Arts, Boston.

Ching or Book of Changes is a divination manual in two parts. The first section consists of rhymed traditional lore, typical of peasant lore throughout the world. The second part is a handbook, depending largely upon interpretation of the *pa kua*, the eight trigrams, to deal with formulae of the kind also associated with the oracle bones mentioned already. The method of employing the *pa kua* is attributed to Wen the father of the first Chou king, Wu. The *Li Chi*, Book of Rites, and the *Chou Li*, Chou Ritual, are both manuals. The latter purports to be a manual of Chou ritual although in fact it was compiled in the third century B.C. when Chou was already a spent force. The *Li Chi* was compiled by Tai the Younger about 50 B.C. but the earliest elements included may date from the time of the

Confucian Analects, that is from before 450 B.C. These are what Karlgren has called systematising texts: their function is not to record but to set out, in the tradition of the Confucian scholars who compiled and reconstructed them, what the rites should be, not what they actually were.

There are other textual sources. Of these one, the *Chhun Chhiu*, Spring and Autumn Annals, is a history of the state of Lu from 722 to 481 B.C. and wrongly attributed by orthodox Confucian scholars to the master himself. The work is a dull but apparently accurately dated chronicle; there is every reason to believe that it was paralleled in all the other states. A rather more lively account of history in the feudal period is to be found in the *Tso Chuan*, which incorporates a brief ritual commentary

on the *Chhun Chhiu*. The *Tso Chuan* is a compilation, attributed to the writer Tso Shih (*c.* 330 B.C.) but in fact a composite work of various dates from about 430 B.C. to the middle of the third century B.C. with amendments and additions attributable to Confucian scholars of Chhin and Han times. This is a valuable source for mythology, but its versions of myths and legends must be treated as the products of Confucian editing.

Other philosophical schools

Of the non-Confucian schools there is very little that has survived from early times. The Legalist school is represented by the *Shang Chun Shu*, the work of a member of the princely house of Wei who flourished in the mid-fourth century B.C., and the philosopher Han Fei Tzu, of the following century. Both these incorporate traditions from the early period of Chinese history which reflect ideas outside the canons of Confucian orthodoxy. Another valuable source for such matters is the work of the Taoist writer Chuang-tzu, who is perhaps best known for his discussion of the problem of knowledge:

> Once Chuang dreamed that he was a butterfly, fluttering about enjoying himself. The butterfly did not know that it was Chuang. Then it awoke and was truly Chuang again. But I do not know whether it was then Chuang dreaming he was a butterfly or whether I am now a butterfly dreaming that I am Chuang.

Those concerned with Chinese mythography must often have somewhat similar sensations of doubt.

The creation of the world

Pottery tomb decorations of the Six Dynasties period (221-581 A.D.), showing female figures riding on the symbolic animals of the four cardinal directions, which grew from the dead Phan-ku and so were ultimately derived from the principles of *yin* and *yang*. The animals themselves came to represent the opposing forces which made up the harmony of the universe, and were associated with seasons, colours and the elements, as well as directions. Nelson Gallery, Kansas City.

Top left. The Green Dragon of the east and of spring, whose element was wood. The dragon, as bringer of regenerating rain, embodied the *yang* principle, positive and male.

Bottom left. The Red Bird of the south, the phoenix or *feng huang*, whose element was fire and whose season was summer. It represented drought and embodied the *yin* principle, negative and female. The phoenix represented the Empress, while the dragon stood for the Emperor.

Top right. The White Tiger of the west, regarded as the king of beasts, whose season was autumn and whose element was metal. In dynastic mythology metallurgy was the key to sovereignty.

Bottom right. The Dark Warrior, a tortoise and a snake, associated with the north and with winter, whose element was water and whose colour was black.

Most, if not all, mythologies include an account of the creation of the world and its inhabitants, both human and animal, together with some explanation of the origins of their natural setting. That such accounts can be found in Chinese is true, but what we have is rudimentary and gives every appearance of being the product of scholarly compilers who were, generally, concerned to recount cosmogonies as parables to illustrate philosophical theories. The most extensive account of the creation, involving a giant called Phan-ku, has survived only in texts from the third to sixth centuries A.D., and there is good reason to think that this story was not incorporated into Chinese tradition until after the assimilation of the southern region. There are, on the other hand, accounts of the structure of the world – rather than of its creation which seems

to have interested the Chinese much less – which are older than the Phan-ku myth and seem to belong to an original Chinese tradition. These we shall consider later, but first we must examine what there is of a creation story.

Order from chaos

Philosophically, for the Chinese as for other people, creation was the act of reducing chaos to order, a theme which persists throughout Chinese thought. For the essence of good rule is that Heaven and Earth shall be in accord and the rites observed. The best known allegory of the ending of Chaos is to be found in the work of Chuang-tzu (third century B.C.) who tells how Hu, the emperor of the Northern Sea, and Shu, the emperor of the Southern Sea, used from time to time to meet half way between their respective domains, on the territory of the emperor of the Centre, Hun-tun. Hun-tun was most hospitable, but was distinguished from other men by the fact that he lacked the seven orifices, for seeing, hearing, eating and breathing. Wishing to repay him for his kindness, Shu and Hu decided that they would bore the necessary holes in Hun-tun and this they did at the rate of one hole a day. But on the seventh day Hun-tun, whose name means Chaos, died. At the same moment the world came into being. There is an interesting additional turn to the story, since the combined names of the two other emperors, Shu-hu, mean lightning, and there is a hint that it is the lightning which strikes Chaos and destroys it so that the world may emerge.

Soymié has noted that in certain ritual transpositions lightning is represented by burning arrows directed at a goatskin bottle which may have represented chaos. There are two curious stories concerned with the fate of the Shang dynasty and the end of the dynastic line where the theme of shooting at a sack is to be found. The first of these con-

cerns King Wu-i, who made a figure in human shape and called it Thien-shen, god of Heaven. He then played *chhi* (a board game of the draughts or checkers type) with the figure, whose pieces were moved by a man appointed to the task by the king. There is no mention of the stake, but the victorious king thereupon mocked and abused the figure. He then made a sack of skin, filled it with blood and, having had it hung up, shot arrows

at it, saying that he was shooting at Heaven. According to the *Shu Ching*, where this story is found, Wu-i subsequently went on a hunting trip, during which he was struck by lightning and killed.

This inevitably recalls the tradition implicit in the story that Shu-hu Lightning destroyed Hun-tun Chaos and thereby brought order into the world. There is some evidence that the popular name for a leather bottle *chhih-i* was *hun-tun* and in view of the fact that, as we shall see below, Hun-tun was sometimes conceived of as a bird, we should note that the word *chhih* means owl.

Hun-tun is also conceived of in human form, as a wicked son of the Yellow Emperor, Huang Ti, who sends him into exile; in other texts there is a tradition that the exiling of Hun-tun was an act of the ruler Shun, just before he handed over power to Yu the Great, the founder of the Hsia dynasty.

Yet another version is to be found in the *Shan Hai Ching*, the Hill and River Classic, where Hun-tun is a mythical bird like a yellow bag. (This links the creature both with Huang Ti, the Yellow Emperor, father of one Hun-tun, and with the idea of Hun-tun as a sack.) At the same time, its colour is red like fire. It has six feet and four wings, but lacks a face – that is, lacks the seven openings. It can dance and can sing despite the absence of a mouth, and lives on the Mountain of the Sky which is rich in ores and in jade. And, because the Yellow Emperor is the emperor of the Centre in various cardinal systems as was Hun-tun in the story with which we started, he too is sometimes considered to be Chaos. In another text Hun-tun is described as lacking the five viscera, although he has a stomach.

A more important tradition, however, links the seven openings with the supposed seven openings of the heart whose possession was the mark of an upright man. It is recorded of Chou Hsin, the last ruler of the Shang dynasty and a paradigm of cruelty and vice that he was reproved by his uncle Prince Pi Kan for his evil government. Chou Hsin replied: 'It is said that you are a sage and I have heard that a sage has seven openings to his heart'. He then had Pi Kan slain and his heart torn out to see whether it was true.

A further point of interest is that the last of Wu-i's lineage, Yen, the feudal prince of Sung, arrogated to himself the title of king. He was finally defeated by the state of Chhi and its allies, Wei and Chhu. And of him we are told by Ssu-ma Chhien that 'he filled a leather bottle with blood, hung it up and shot arrows against it, saying that he was shooting at Heaven'. With his defeat in 282 B.C. the last vestiges of Shang power came to an end. Now in recounting the fate of Yen, Ssu-ma Chhien recalled the story of Wu-i (as well as that of Chieh, the tyrannical last ruler of Hsia). This seems to indicate that it was the presumption of challenging Heaven which led to the defeat (or destruction) of Yen as it had to that of his remote ancestor Wu-i. According to Granet, Heaven in Chinese thought is also a symbol for the people:

the implication then would seem to be that both Yen and Wu-i fell because they were oppressive rulers. It seems more likely, however, that it was their attempts to seize supreme power within a feudal system which incurred the displeasure of their fellow princes.

According to a text of the third century A.D., Chaos was like a hen's egg. At this time neither Earth nor Heaven existed. From this egg, Phan-ku was born. The parts of the egg separated, the heavy elements forming the Earth, and the light, pure ones the Sky. These were *yin* and *yang*. For a period of eighteen thousand years the distance between earth and sky increased by ten feet daily and Phan-ku grew at the same rate, so that his body always filled the space between the two. Despite this, when Phan-ku is represented, it is as a dwarf clad either in a bearskin or in leaves. On his death, the various parts of his body became different natural elements, though the exact details of these changes

Left. Cosmological chart showing strong Indian influence but preserving the Chinese notion of a chariot-like universe, with a central support and subsidiary guy ropes. British Museum.

Phan-ku, bearing in his hands the egg of Chaos, which is composed of the symbols of *yin* and *yang*, and from which he was born. Phan-ku lived for eighteen thousand years, growing at the rate of ten feet a day and filling the space between Heaven and Earth. Nineteenth-century lithograph. British Museum.

The fairy Ma-ku, who lived in the second century A.D. She was a beneficent sorceress who reclaimed from the sea a large area of the coast of Kiangsu and converted it into a mulberry orchard. In another avatar she took pity on her father's labourer, quarrelling with her father as a result and fleeing to the mountains to become a hermit. Painting by Hsiang Kun. British Museum.

The Four Kings of Hell, who correspond to the
Four Diamond Kings of Heaven in Buddhist belief
Other systems held that there were ten hells, or
even fourteen — each with its own king but under
the control of Yen-lo. They guarded the register of
judgments which Monkey stole when he was
carried off to Hell. Anonymous painting. British
Museum.

The lower part of the universe in design, showing the animals and elements of the four cardinal directions surrounding the square earth, which is lapped on all four sides by the primeval ocean in which it floats. Bronze marriage mirror of the Thang dynasty, probably early eighth century A.D. Seattle Art Museum.

vary from text to text and from period to period. Thus in Han or even slightly earlier sources, his head became the Mountain of the East, his stomach the Mountain of the Centre, his left arm that of the South, his right arm that of the North and his feet that of the West. Another source derives all the cardinal mountains from his head and makes the sun and moon from his eyes, the rivers and seas from his flesh, the plants from his hair. Other theoreticians explained that his tears were the course of rivers and seas, his breath the wind, his eyes lightning and his voice thunder. Yet another story explained changes in the weather by changes in his mood. The most detailed version of this process of transformation is even more specific. His breath became wind and clouds, his voice thunder and lightning; his left eye was the sun, his right the moon; from his body the cardinal points and the five great mountains derived, while his blood and bodily fluids made the rivers and seas and his nervous and venous systems the layers of the earth. The fields and soil were the transformation of his flesh. The hairs of his head and eyebrows became the stars and planets, while metals and stones were the products of his teeth and bones; his semen became pearls, his bone marrow jade. His sweat was the rain and the fleas on his body became the human race.

These stories are late in the versions in which we have them and it is likely that the tradition of their southern origin is basically correct, though there are elements in them which seem to fit the cosmogony of Chuang-tzu. Chaos must end before the world begins. Similarly the concept of a pillar which keeps apart (or joins) the two parts of the world is found in Chinese cosmographical systems. There is also a tradition that there was a communicating link between Heaven and Earth until Shang Ti ordered Chhung-li, a culture hero, to destroy it. The separation of chaos into an initial *yin* and *yang* is to be found as a fundamental concept in Chinese thought, perhaps reflected in a tradition

from the region around the Yangtze delta that *yin* and *yang* derive from Phanku and his wife. There is some indication, though it is very imprecise, that at one time *yin* and *yang*, which are generally thought of as classificatory categories or abstract cosmic forces, may have had a more concrete form. There is a single reference to them as *shen* deities, responsible for the management of Earth and Heaven.

The concept of the world egg is not confined to China, nor that of the primordial being from whom all else is derived. In classical Indian cosmogonies a world egg occurs which opens to form the heavens from its upper part, earth from its lower. Brahma, the creator,

Yi arriving on his twice-monthly visit to the moon, where his wife Heng-o lived in the Palace of Great Cold which he built for her out of cinnamon trees. Though Heng-o had stolen the pill of immortality, Yi too obtained immortality, but had to live separately, in the Palace of the Sun or Palace of the Lonely Park. Heng-o represented the cold, female principle of *yin*, while Yi represented the warm, male principle of *yang*. Korean mirror of the Koryo period (A.D. 936-1392).

Stylised tortoise, a symbol of stability, holding up the foundations of the universe. Originally a link between Heaven and Earth, the pillar was later thought to keep them apart. Probably *c.* eighteenth century A.D. Based on a Ming style. Fogg Art Museum, Cambridge, Mass.

emerged from this egg, and by incantation produced eight celestial elephants from part of the egg, to stand at the quarters and the four mid-points to hold earth and sky apart. There is also an Indian tradition, recorded in a very late hymn of the *Rig Veda*, that the whole of creation derives from the primordial giant, Purusha, who is also the sacrifice of the gods. The Brahmin caste emerged from his mouth, the Kshatriya (warrior) caste from his arms, the Vaisya (merchants) from his thighs, the Sudra from his feet. From him also some of the gods were born, while from his navel came the air, from his head the sky and from his ears the four quarters. Though one story in the *Upanishads* states that the creature from which all emerged was a sacrificial horse, another upanishadic source has a single creator, a male, who divided himself into a male and female self. Approaching his female self he begat men. Then the creative pair assumed the forms of all creatures in turn and begat each of them. One is reminded of the Chinese version of creation in which Thien-lung and Ti-ya are the origin of all creation, as we shall discuss below. It is not possible to say whether these parallels are the result of direct influences between India and China or represent traditions deriving from a common source. It should be noted, however, that many of the Chinese stories are late and may owe something to the Indian influences at the time when Buddhist pilgrims and scholars maintained contact with Indian intellectual circles.

We have already mentioned a tradition that when Phan-ku was happy the weather was fine, but when he grew angry the weather changed to fit his mood. There is a considerably more complicated account of the origins of climatic change, the cycle of seasons and day and night to be found in the *Shan Hai Ching.* A monster Kung Kung, (p. 85), having failed in an attempt to seize power from one of the Five Emperors, in his fury impaled Mount Pu Chou on his horn. His attempt to destroy the world also failed, but the damage to the mountain which was the

Li, the Governor of Fire, riding on a tiger. Also known as Chu-jung, who presided over the south, he helped to break the link between Heaven and Earth and thereafter was appointed to keep men in their appointed positions in the universal order. Horniman Museum.

Right. Yao, the fourth of the Five Emperors who taught mankind the arts of civilisation. The sons of the Five Emperors were considered unworthy to inherit the throne. Yao's throne therefore passed to Shun; the upheaval occasioned by this was so violent that all ten suns appeared together and, but for Yi the Good Archer, would have destroyed the world. Painting by Ma Lin. Sung dynasty. National Museum of Taiwan.

A *pi*, symbol of the circular sky or Heaven. The hole in the centre corresponds to the *lie-chhiu* through which the lightning flashes. From Chou times onwards the *pi* was used in ritual by the king, called the 'Son of Heaven' because provided he remained virtuous Heaven bestowed on him its mandate to rule on earth. This *pi*, decorated with a 'grain pattern', may have been used for the investiture of a prince. Huan ritual object. National Museum of Taiwan.

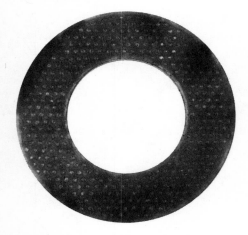

A jade *tsung*, symbol of the square earth, whose central cylinder may originally have been designed to hold ancestral tablets, perhaps in the form of phallic symbols. Carved in incorruptible jade, *tsungs* were in burials placed on the stomach of the deceased, the stomach of Phan-ku being the origin of the Mountain of the Centre, the fifth 'direction', whose colour was yellow and whose element was earth. Han dynasty. Rietbergmuseum, Zurich.

north-west pillar of the world tore a hole in the sky. In the absence of sky, the sun is unable to shine there, and instead there is a flaming dragon. This creature has a human face and a dragon's body a thousand *li* in length. Its colour is red, its eyes fixed. When its eyes are open it is day; when they are closed it is night. Its exhalation is winter; its inhalation is summer. When it stops breathing there is neither rain nor wind; when it resumes breathing the wind blows. It neither eats nor drinks. To the story of Kung Kung we return in the next section, for it is more properly concerned with the structure of the cosmos. What is interesting here is to see how the consequences of Kung Kung's act are used as a logical base for another, quite different story which 'explains' another set of phenomena.

The creation of man

Although Chinese mythology has little to say on creation in general – cosmogonies do not appear to have interested those who preserved early traditions or the scholars who speculated upon so much else – it might be expected that the creation of man himself would have seemed a theme of more importance. But this is not the case. We have already noted a late story, almost certainly a literary invention, that men were born of the parasites upon the body of the dead Phan-ku. The only other legend of any extent concerned with human creation presents the creator as the goddess Nu-kua, who is sometimes treated as the wife of Fu-hsi (see p. 86), and who as a divine being attempted to repair the damage done by Kung Kung. According to a Han dynasty text, once Heaven and Earth had separated, there were still no men. Nu-kua set about modelling these out of yellow earth. But this process seemed too tedious and so the goddess took a rope and dipped it into the mud and trailed it about so that drops fell off. From the modelled specimens came the noble and the rich, while those who dripped from the muddy rope were the humble and the poor.

A folktale of quite uncertain date, re-

corded in Hopei, succeeds in conflating the idea of Phan-ku as the origin if not the creator of man and that of Nu-kua as the creator. In this story, once Earth and Heaven, plants and animals had sprung up, Phan-ku was dissatisfied because there was no reasoning being who could develop and utilise other living creatures, these being incapable of any action on their own account. He therefore set about modelling men and women in clay. This took him a whole day. As soon as they were dry, they were impregnated with *yin* and *yang* and became human beings. Phan-ku had made a large supply which was baking in the sun when dark clouds appeared in the north-west (the region where the sun was unable to shine in the Kung Kung story). Fearful that his day's work might be wasted, Phan-ku heaped up the figures and carried them indoors on an iron fork. But a great storm burst before he got them into safety and some were damaged. That is why there are crippled and defective people on earth.

There are other stories in which men are the product of sexual intercourse between a couple – often incestuous. Nu-kua herself is treated as a brother-sister pair in one version. Another couple, attendants of the god of Literature Wen-chhang, are Thien-lung and Ti-ya, who is also known as Ti-mu (that is, Earth-mother). From the union of this last couple not only men but all creation are said to have emerged.

The structure of the physical world

From sources which in the main date from the later part of the Han dynasty we can reconstruct some notion of the ideas which pre-Chhin cosmographers entertained about the structure of the universe. Of the three cosmographical schools which appear to have existed, one called *suan ye* has left no body of doctrine, though it is known that its followers did not believe that the sky was solid, but that the sun and other heavenly bodies moved freely about in it. Of the other two schools considerably more is known and it will be no surprise to learn that the views which they held were completely incompatible.

One, which seems to show signs of a connection with the Phan-ku myth, went by the name of *hun-thien* and conceived of the world as a hen's egg with the long axis as the vertical. The upper part of the shell had the sky on its inner surface across which the stars moved. The earth floated upon the primeval ocean which lay in the bottom of the shell. Tidal influences accounted for the earth's seasons. There is no elaboration of the details about the ocean.

It seems most likely that the third school represented the oldest tradition or certainly one older than the *hun-thien* concept. For the supporters of this third school, known as *thien-kai* or *chou-pei*, the sky was an inverted bowl rotating on its own axis above the earth. The axis was the Pole Star, which carried with it the other stars fixed to the surface of the bowl. The earth was a flat surface or a truncated four-sided pyramid with the four seas set one on each of its sides. The notion of the earth's surface as square is old in the Chinese system of writing, while the term for space defined by the cardinal points *yang* also means square. The sun (or its deity) is represented by a square mound; the capital is square, as is the royal domain, and space can be seen as squares fitting about one another over a common centre or as juxtaposed lesser squares related to minor centres. Earth is still and square, while the round sky revolves: the *yang* sky contrasts with the *yin* earth.

The bowl of the *chou-pei* system was conceived of as solid: when Kung Kung attacked it he tore a hole so that the sun could no longer visit the north-west section. Such a substantial bowl required supports, and these supports in their turn required guy ropes to brace them. These fastenings are called by the same name as the lashings which fix the chariot platform to the chassis. Metaphors relating the structure of the world to a chariot are common: *thien-kai* itself refers to the umbrella over the chariot. The sky is considered as the umbrella on its pole, the earth as the body of the chariot; sometimes the sky

此是關聖帝君神像夜讀春秋
側立周倉手持偃月刀軍民人
供之

is considered as a chariot wheel in a horizontal plane with the Pole Star at its hub. The ancient Chinese chariot had a square body with a circular upper part supported by a single shaft. But although the chariot metaphor implied a central support, it is more common to find that the sky is supported by four or eight pillars, without any attempt being made to explain how such a system allowed for the revolution of the heavenly bodies.

On the other hand, the obvious discrepancy between the Pole Star as a theoretical centre, which has also to be the centre of the kingdom, itself *Chhung kuo* – the Middle Kingdom, and the actual, off-centre position of this star is explained by the myth of Kung Kung. For when he impaled Mount Pu Chou on his horn, the mountain broke and as a result the sky collapsed in the north-west. The heavenly bodies tipped towards the break, while the earth tilted the other way, towards the south-east. And because of this the waters flowed south-eastwards. The name of the mountain means Not-circular. It seems most likely that the name refers both to the breaking of the circle of supporting pillars and to the breaching of whatever retained the waters. For the floods which followed Kung Kung's attack were themselves the subject of a series of myths to which we shall return.

THE SEPARATION OF HEAVEN AND EARTH

In the story of the cosmic egg Phan Ku's body acts as a link between Heaven and Earth as well as being the column that keeps them apart. In other cosmographies also there are columns which serve this dual function. But it seems that this link was a mixed blessing and according to the *Shu Ching* the order was given to Chhung-li, or to Chhung and Li, to break the communication between Earth and Heaven so that there was no descending or ascending. Another text gives a more or less full explanation of this curious occurrence. When Chuan Hu succeeded Shao Hao as emperor, he found that during his predecessor's reign the Nine Li had caused confusion between gods and men;

there was no proper order in the sacrifices since men and gods held the same positions. So Chuan Hu ordered Chhung, the Governor of the south, to preside over Heaven and organise the gods in their proper order, and Li, the Governor of fire, to do the same for men. This broke the communications between Earth and Heaven. In the *Tso Chuan* Shao Hao, the successor to Huang Ti, had a younger brother Chhung who was made a deity called Kou Mang to preside over the element wood and over the east. Li was the son of Chuan Hu and was the deity Chu-jung who presided over fire and the south.

Whatever we may make of these stories, two points seem worthy of note. The first is that without order, nothing can function. An important element in Chinese religion and ritual is concerned with methods of establishing and maintaining order. Secondly, we see here the beginning of the complex bureaucracy which in evolved religious systems was to grow into a pantheon organised just like the imperial bureaucracy with departments to control every aspect and activity of the world, whether good or evil, approved or disapproved.

The heavenly bodies

In view of the general lack of cosmological and cosmographical myths it will be no surprise that Chinese myths relating to the sun, moon and stars are sketchy and generally inconsistent. There is a hole in the top of the sky called *Lie-chhiu*, through which the lightning flashes. Beyond this there is nothing. Similarly there is a horizontal gap between earth and sky and beyond this a void. Sun, moon and stars are inside the earth-sky complex. There is some evidence, of considerable antiquity, to suggest that sun and moon are related through a common father, the emperor Shun. Both sun and moon are in fact suns and moons, ten and twelve in number respectively. Each of these heavenly bodies is in the care of a mother who is in some sense responsible for their proper functioning. The traditions relating to these functions we may now consider.

SOLAR MYTHS

There are ten suns which appear in turn in the sky. They are conveyed across it in a chariot drawn by dragons and driven by their mother. In the early morning the duty sun emerges from the Valley of Light and is bathed by its mother in the lake which borders the valley on the extreme eastern edge of the world. By the lake there is an enormous tree, *fu-sang*, which is also called *po* or *khung-sang*, hollow mulberry. Newly bathed, all ten suns mount into the tree; but while nine lodge in its lower branches, the tenth climbs to the very top. From here it sets out upon its chariot ride across the sky, continuing until it reaches Mount Yen-tzu in the far west, where the dragons can be unyoked. Here too there seems to be a lake and a tree called *jo*. The manner in which the duty sun returns from west to east is nowhere discussed, but it seems probable that it descends to earth by way of the tree, whose flowers are red and glow by night, and are perhaps the stars of the night sky. Some mention is made of stages upon the east-west journey,

which are, in fact, the daylight hours.

Once again, the story fails to fit the observable facts of solar behaviour and so two further characters seem to have been introduced into the story to explain the discrepancies. These deities located at the north-east and north-west corners of the world control two of the winds and are in some sense responsible for the course of both sun and moon and the seasonal variations in the length of their courses. This element in the story is late, however, and does not seem to belong to the original myth with the two trees, which is certainly old. It is interesting to note the evidence for this in the ideograms. From earliest times the character for east has consisted of a sun in a tree. The character for light is of a sun above a tree, while that for darkness shows a sun under a tree. It is also interesting to observe that dawn is written with the elements nine and sun, for it is at this moment that the duty sun mounts into the sky while its nine brothers lodge in the branches of the *po* tree.

From time to time more than one

Right. Heng-o, goddess of the moon. She was the younger sister of Ho Po, Count of the River. When Yi the Divine Archer was sent by Yao to stop the river flooding in Kaoliang he shot and injured the spirit responsible for the flooding, but spared Heng-o who accompanied him, merely aiming his arrow to lodge in her hair. In gratitude, Hengo-o became his wife. Modern terracotta statuette. Musée Guimet.

An early stone-rubbing showing one of the ten suns crossing the heavens from the hollow mulberry tree, *khung-sang*, in the east, to the *po*-tree in the west. The chariot in which the sun is conveyed has the circular canopy over a square chassis which characterised the shape of the Chinese universe.

sun is said to have appeared in the sky. This sign of ill-omen predicates above all the fall of a dynasty. The victory of Yin, or Shang, over Hsia was preceded by the appearance of three suns, that of Chou over Yin-Shang by two. This last phenomenon is explained as the appearance in the east of the new sun, Chou, soon to replace the setting, western sun of Shang. In political allegory a disloyal and rebellious minister is said to attack the hollow mulberry tree, which is the place from which the rising sun (and the new emperor) sets out upon its journey.

The most celebrated occasion when multiple suns were to be seen was when Yao was about to lose his throne to Shun; for all ten suns appeared at once so that their heat threatened all life upon earth. The emperor Shun gave a magic bow to Yi the Good Archer, who shot nine suns from the sky to leave but one for the future. The sun is made of fire, it is *yang* and in its breast is a three-footed raven. When Yi saved the world the ravens fell to the earth.

Yi is of interest in another connection for he is the husband of Heng-o, who stole from him the drug of immortality which he had obtained from Hsi Wang Mu, the ruler of the Western Paradise. After the theft his wife fled to the moon, where she dwells as the celestial toad.

LUNAR MYTHS

Of the lunar myths even less has survived. There are twelve moons which certainly represent the twelve lunar months. These travel across the sky by chariot from the west after being bathed in a western lake, but the charioteer is unspecified. No details of the journey survive, but the moon is made of water and is *yin*. (Moon and sun are quintes-

sentially *yin* and *yang*.) The creature that inhabits, the moon is either a hare (to which the references are earlier) or a toad. By Han times it was generally accepted that both hare and toad lived together on the moon. A splendid Thang mirror shows one resolution of the problem, for on it the hare is already on the moon and preparing the elixir of immortality which Heng-o is to drink to become an immortal toad, shown near the foot of the Cassia tree, which is also on the moon.

THE STARS

In general sky and stellar myths belong to a later period of Chinese mythology when the heavenly bureaucracy was well established. It will therefore be convenient to consider these later. But there is one well-known story to which reference is certainly made in the *Shih Ching* and which has survived in popular tradition, undoubtedly because of its romantic content. For the cultural historian its interest lies in the apparent preservation of an early period in Chinese prehistory during which men and women formed two distinct socio-economic groups within the community. These groups held rituals in spring and autumn and were the occasions for betrothals, weddings and, probably, ritualised sexual licence. There is some evidence to suggest that the myth in its original form referred to a matrilocal society, but as it has survived the heroine goes to her husband's home.

The story relates to two groups of three stars in the constellations of Aquila and Lyra which lie on opposite sides of the Milky Way, the Celestial River. They are known as the Celestial Cowherd and the Heavenly Weaver-girl. During all the year the couple, who were once married and lived together in amorous dalliance to the neglect of their duties, are forced to attend to their respective tasks; but on the seventh day of the seventh month the girl is free to cross the Milky Way by a bridge of magpies and go to her husband the Cowherd. Should it rain then the birds will seek shelter, and in the absence of the bridge the Weaver must spend another year of separation from her husband.

Earth, water and wind

We have seen in the preceding chapter the little that has survived of Chinese traditions about the creation of the physical world. We must now consider how the Chinese conceived the world in which they lived. Theoretically, the land was surrounded by sea, which lay on each of its four sides. (In some systems the land also floated upon the primeval ocean.) In fact, as a glance at the map shows, China has an immensely long eastern coastline; but, as we have already seen, the 'Chinese' did not reach the coast, and probably did not even know of its existence, during the period in which many of the basic ideas of Chinese traditional belief were established. It is therefore tempting to see in the idea of a surrounding ocean a simple result of logical analysis: the earth was four-sided; the rain ran off to each of the sides; therefore there was a sea on each side of the land.

The Eastern Sea

There was no problem of overflowing for far to the east in the Eastern Sea (the real sea which was itself mysterious and magical, as we shall learn below) there was a hole without bottom into which all the waters, of the rain, of the rivers and of the sea, as well as those of the Han of the Sky, the Milky Way, poured without cease. What happened to them after that we are not told. And in the neighbourhood of this mystical overflow were the islands of Pheng-lai, a paradise inhabited by feathered and winged Immortals.

There were five islands to begin with each floating freely without anchor. Here there flourished the herb of immortality which was the staple of the inhabitants and in search of which emperors were to send fleets into the Eastern Sea. Because they were not anchored the islands used to drift around in the ocean until they bumped against the mainland of China. This upset the Immortals, who complained to the Celestial Emperor.

THE GOD OF THE SEA AND THE OCEAN WIND

He ordered Yu-chhiang, the god of the ocean wind, to fix the islands in place by attaching them to large tortoises, three to each island – one to hold the island in place while the other two were in waiting. Each period of duty lasted sixty thousand years.

This worked well until a giant from the realm of the Count of Dragons, bent on fishing, strode into the sea and reached the islands in a few steps. At his first cast he caught six tortoises, and the two islands which they had anchored drifted away northwards and sank. The enraged Emperor of Heaven reduced all giants in size (though they remained sufficiently large to be intimidating); the three islands whose tortoises were still in place stayed in position to attract seekers after immortality.

In the *Shan Hai Ching* Yu-chhiang is a wind-god (but not the wind-god who is the Count of the Wind) with a bird's body and a human face. There are green serpents at his head and feet. He lives in the north or the north-west where he is god of the ocean wind. But he is also a sea-god. In this form he has the body of a fish with human hands and feet, and he rides upon two dragons. The body is that of a northern whale, *kun*, of vast size. When the whale grows angry it changes into a giant bird, *pheng*, which rises from the sea, its body stirring up great waves. The sky is darkened by the spread of its wings as it flies southwards for six months till it comes to rest in the sea of the south. In this legend we have some attempt to present the wind system of the China Sea with its monsoon pattern.

An account of the *pheng* is found in Chuang-tzu, where we learn that it is the *kun* (several thousand *li* in breadth and of unknown length) in another form. Its back is like Thai Shan and its wings like the clouds all round the sky. When it moves south it flaps its wings on the water for 3,000 *li* and then mounts on a whirlwind, as on the whorls of a goat's horns, for 90,000 *li*, 'till, far removed from the cloudy vapours, it bears on its back the blue sky, and then it shapes its course for the South, and proceeds to the ocean there'. For Chuang-tzu this legend prompts a moral observation:

A quail by the side of a marsh

Left. One of the Eight Immortals, a group of Taoist holy men who were not connected in life but who in various ways all gained the right to feast on the fruit of immortality at the Peach Festival of Hsi Wang Mu. Porcelain. Sixteenth century A.D.

Bottom left. Porcelain plate depicting a carp attempting to leap the Lungmen Falls or Dragon Gate on the Yellow River at the border between Shensi and Shansi provinces. Once a year all the fish competed in this attempt, those which succeeded being transformed immediately into dragons and rising up into the sky. Dragons are said to rise to the skies in spring and to plunge into the waters in autumn. Reign of Khang Hsi. Victoria and Albert Museum.

Bottom right. The lid of a *hun-phing*, or urn of the soul, a type of ritual vessel modelled in the shape of a fairy mountain with subsidiary peaks and designed to emit the vapours exhaled by all living nature. The summit is square, like the earth, while the base is lapped by waters. Khun-lun was conceived as such a mountain. Yueh ware, porcelain. Third century A.D. Cleveland Museum of Art.

Right. The Protector against Hail and Master of Thunder, who was especially worshipped by cultivators. As can be seen from his hammer and chisel he was a smith and thus, after the pattern of Yu, a controller of weather and of imperial power in rivalry with the Son of Heaven. Victoria and Albert Museum.

The Western Paradise of Khun-lun as depicted on a Buddhist scroll. Buddha sits enthroned and surrounded by his court of celestial beings. Indian influence led to the identification of Khun-lun with the Hindu Sumeru, so that this Buddhist paradise is surrounded by waters, which gave immortality.

laughed at it and said: where is it going to? I spring up with a bound and come down again when I have reached but a few fathoms, and then fly about among the brushwood and bushes; and this is the perfection of flying. Where is that creature going to?

This, remarks the philosopher, shows the difference between the small and the great.

The *pheng* occurs in later Chinese sources as a creature of the African coast, its home being in the neighbourhood of Zanzibar. According to a writer on twelfth to thirteenth century A.D. trade, the bird was so vast that as it rose into the air the sun was obscured momentarily. It could swallow a camel; its quills were so big that they could be used for water containers. There can be little doubt that the *pheng* is here conflated with the roc, of which Marco Polo wrote that it could swallow an elephant.

THE COUNT OF THE WIND

The true wind-god or Count of the Wind is known either as Feng Po or as Fei Lien. Though he too has connections with the sea, he is chiefly associated with the sky. He is said to be under the jurisdiction of the star Chhi in the constellation Sagittarius, because the winds are strong as the moon leaves the house of Sagittarius. The winds themselves are in a great sack from whose mouth the Count directs them in whichever direction he wills. Before becoming controller of the winds, Fei Lien had been a minister of the tyrannical Chou and was famed for his speed of walking. As a divinity he is associated with drought because the winds can parch all vegetation and dry out the soil just as much as they can bring the rain-loaded clouds.

In another story Fei Lien was a supporter of Chhih-yu, who rebelled against Huang Ti. Being transformed into a monster for his crime, he revenged himself by causing great storms in the south. The emperor Yao, a successor to Huang Ti, sent the Divine Archer to restore order. The latter ordered the people to spread before their houses a great cloth, fixed with stones, to divert the wind so that he might ride upon it to the top of a mountain. From here he saw the wind in the shape of a great sack of yellow and white material which heaved in and out gustily. He shot an arrow at it, whereupon the monster took refuge in a deep cave and drew its sword to ward off the Divine Archer. The latter fired a second arrow wounding the monster in the knee, whereupon it surrendered. From that time forward the winds were operated in a proper manner.

Sometimes Fei Lien is described as a bird-dragon, with a bird's body and the head of a stag, his tail that of a serpent. In anthropomorphic form Feng Po is an old man with a white beard, red and blue cap and yellow cloak. Sometimes the winds are attributed to an old woman, Feng Pho-pho, who can be seen riding her tiger upon the clouds. The mountains were recognised as being closely associated with climatic phenomena. On the mountain of the east, Thai Shan, there lived in the form of a white-headed, one-eyed bull with a serpent's tail a creature called Fei – readily confused with the wind-deity Fei Lien who died and was buried upon Huo Thai Shan. His tread dried up rivers or parched growing plants. Clearly we have here another mountain dwelling wind-deity.

The cardinal mountains

According to the Chinese cosmology the earth had four cardinal mountains, to which a fifth was added to represent the centre point. It is this pattern which is the most significant in classical Chinese thought, for these mountains played a major part in the old Chinese imperial ritual. Human activity was set within a square frame, just as the earth was square: the cardinal mountains were in relation to this frame, as were the gates to the (square) city. The ruler toured the four mountains to take possession of his realm: the vassals were represented by a person or persons called Four-Mountains whose presence at court after the tour of the four cardinal peaks symbolically completed this possession. Of these cardinal points one alone seems consistently to have occupied the attention of the rulers, while a second mountain which was not strictly a member of this group steadily increased in importance until it almost came to dominate. In the east Thai Shan; in the west Khun-lun.

THAI SHAN

Thai Shan was the mountain from which the sun on duty began its journey across the sky. By Han times the souls of the dead were thought to return to a region at the foot of the mountain, while the mountain, in a personified form, became an arbiter of destiny and death. Even when the full structure of the Buddhist afterworld with all its apparatus for the disposal of the dead became established in China, the concept of a Thai Shan Hades nevertheless still

The five cardinal points represented by their emblematic figures in hunting and battle scenes. The Five Mountains were the source of power (thus the dynastic swords were made from ores collected from them and swords were hidden in the mountains), and blood sacrifice upheld their power. Pottery tile of the Han dynasty. Musée Cernuschi.

persisted among Chinese of all sects.

POWER THROUGH SACRIFICE

In the seventh century B.C. to sacrifice upon Thai Shan was thought to be the prerogative of a ruler. It seems likely that this idea was native to the region around the mountain itself for the *Chhun Chhiu*, Spring and Autumn Annals, refers to this in connection with the ruler of a state just to the north of the mountain. The first emperor of all China, Shih Huang Ti, wished to make such a sacrifice only after the absorption of the eastern regions; but his ambition remained unfulfilled, for storms drove him from the peak. Perhaps Fei was responsible; but the Han commentators, anxious to exalt the merits of their own dynasty, explained that only sages of supreme merit could carry out such a sacrifice.

The Han emperor Wu was about to re-enact the sacrifices *feng* and *shan*, those to Heaven and Earth, on Thai Shan's peak; but though the claim was that the sacrifices were traditional, those repositories of tradition, the Confucian scholars, were unable to describe the rites involved. It is perhaps significant that the emperor Wu, when he was to make the sacrifices, turned to the magicians, who may well have retained the true rituals in their traditions. They were, in any case, most likely to have known the essentials of what seems to have been a local rite.

The essence of the act was to take possession of territory, a fact which lends colour to the view that the spirit of a territory resides in its central mountain or in its artificial surrogate, the phallic

symbol of a soil-deity. It is interesting, therefore, to note that in 119 B.C., before the emperor Wu made his ascent of Thai Shan, his general Ho Chu-phing had celebrated the conquest of eighty barbarian chiefs by the ascent of Lang-ku-su and Hu-yen to make the sacrifices *feng* and *shan*, apparently to confirm the validity of his occupation of their territories. Such a sacrifice performed by the emperor was, however, not to be undertaken lightly, for the commentators implied that Shih Huang Ti had died prematurely as a result of his failure to complete the ritual once he had ascended the mountain. (He had been rejected by Heaven, though the rejection, it should be noted, took place ten years after the abortive ceremony.) The emperor Wu set out upon his

mission to inspect the east and to sacrifice in 110 B.C. He first performed a sacrifice at the foot of the mountain. This, a public ceremony, was to the Earth. He then ascended the mountain accompanied by Ho Shan, the son of Ho Chu-phing. What took place on the peak was not reported for Ho Shan died immediately after the descent in circumstances which make it obvious that he was disposed of on the emperor's instructions. Wu made two further ascents of Thai Shan, unaccompanied, in 106 and 98 B.C. On all three occasions the weather remained auspiciously calm and fair.

There were complicated family links between the emperor and Ho Shan through the female line in marriage and it seems likely that his presence there was thought a necessary part of

The Five Holy Mountains – those of the four cardinal directions together with the mountain of the Centre. The five mountains were associated with the five elements and thus with the whole mystical system of the Chinese and, as a group, played a central part in dynastic ritual. Yu was said to have discovered that the four cardinal mountains were laid out in an exact square. National Museum of Taiwan.

Supernatural being, possibly Four-Mountains, guardian of the four quarters of the universe, and counsellor of Yao, one of the Five Emperors. His presence at court symbolised the emperor's possession of his realm. Glazed earthenware figure from a tomb. Thang dynasty. Victoria and Albert Museum.

the rites to take possession of the empire by associating matrilineage with the act. The sacrifice at the foot of the mountain was a necessary preliminary to that on the peak though it did not have to take place in such close proximity to it. It was the sacrifice to the Earth *shan* and seems to have been designed to transfer the ownership of the soil to another from whom it might then be reclaimed; the recipient belonged to the wife's group and might possibly be sacrificed himself at the conclusion of the ceremonies.

The rituals of the New Year ended with the quartering of victims at the four gates of the city, another form of integration of the four parts of the realm. There is an ancient tradition that each emperor wished to disembarrass himself of the realm by handing it to another who then committed suicide, a real case of self-sacrifice.

SMITHS AND THE DYNASTIC MOUNTAINS

Perhaps the best known sacrifices to effect some special operation are those which concern sword-making. A series of texts recounts the forging of magic swords, usually to serve as dynastic palladia. These seem to have originated in the region about the mouth of the Yangtze, in the kingdoms of Wu and Yueh. It is probable that they were originally Indonesian stories, at the time when the coastal strip was inhabited by Indonesian-speaking peoples, for there are traces of similar stories in somewhat etiolated form to be found in medieval Javanese dynastic histories.

A basic version of the story is given in the *Wu Yueh Chhun Chhiu*. This tells how Ho Liu, king of Wu, commissioned a pair of swords from the smith Kan Chiang and his wife Mo Yeh. They set out to the Five Mountains to collect suitable ores and then, at an auspicious moment, began the work of making the swords. But at the end of three months the metal had still not been extracted from the ore: the essence of the iron would not melt and flow. Mo Yeh asked her husband why this was. He replied that he did not understand the principle, though he remembered that in similar circumstances his master and the latter's wife had cast themselves into the furnace in order that the work should be accomplished. Then Mo Yeh threw her nail-parings and hair-clippings into the furnace and, after the bellows had been reapplied and more fuel added to the furnace, the swords were successfully made. The male sword was called Kan Chiang, the female Mo Yeh. The smith hid the male sword and gave the female one to the king. On testing the sword, the latter realised that he had been cheated and in his wrath he killed the smith. Kan Chiang, as he died, told his pregnant wife that his death would be avenged by their unborn son and disclosed to her the hiding place of the male sword.

When the son was old enough, his mother told him the story and he went to seek the sword. Having found it, he used it to decapitate himself. A stranger then appeared and took both the sword and the head of Kan Chiang's son to the king, who threw the head into a cauldron in order to melt it. When it failed to melt, the stranger persuaded the king to allow his own head to be cut off in order that it, by falling into the cauldron, should make the first head melt. But when the king's head fell into the cauldron nothing happened. Finally the stranger beheaded himself, and as his head fell into the cauldron all three fused together into a single lump. This was buried at the tumulus of the Three Kings. In some later versions of this story Mo Yeh actually threw herself into the furnace in order that the metal should flow from the ore.

We are told that Kan Chiang hid the male sword in the mountains; this connection between mountains and swords is to be found elsewhere, also in a context that relates to the exercise of suzerainty (and, incidentally, of blood sacrifice). According to the *Che Ya*, certain swords of Yueh were buried in order that they might acquire transcendental power. Once a year they were sprinkled with the blood of humans and of horses. At the time of rain their magical nature manifested itself in their attempts to escape from their sheaths,

Figure of a supernatural creature with monster head, elephant's ears, wings and cloven hooves – the sort of hybrid animal which was supposed to guard the entrances to Khun-lun, palace of the Lord of the Sky. Such figures were placed in tombs to guard them, or perhaps to lead the soul to the Khun-lun paradise. Glazed earthenware. Thang dynasty. Victoria and Albert Museum.

The spirits of the blessed gathering outside the golden ramparts of Hsi Wang Mu's palace on Khun-lun, which can be seen emerging from the clouds. All who approach the court of the Royal Mother of the Western Paradise hope to partake of the fruits of immortality. Anonymous painting. Eighteenth century. British Museum.

when they emitted a metallic sound. Chao Tho, king of Yueh, buried swords of high repute in order to rule the famous mountains of his realm. That is why the mountains of Kwangtung and Kwangsi sometimes see the gleam of swords reflected in the midnight sky. Thus the sword is both a palladium and, it seems likely, an instrument in the king's apparatus for rain-making. This is not surprising, for there is considerable evidence in Chinese sources to suggest that, after the pattern of Yu, the smiths, makers of dynastic swords and challengers therefore of the imperial power, were also masters of the Thunder, controllers of the Seasons, and as ministers rivals before Heaven of the emperor himself. That to forge a pair of swords was to deal in matters of magical power is clearly shown in a story recorded in various Chinese sources, though it is attributed once more to Yueh peoples.

There was once a barbarian chieftain called Fan Chhuei (his personal name means 'Hammer') who had a slave called Fan Wen. One day when the latter was pasturing his master's sheep on the mountainside he found two carp in a stream. He hid them, intending to return later and eat the fish by himself. But his master learned of his find and ordered him to fetch the fish. Fan Wen, ashamed and frightened, claimed that he found two sharpening-stones, not fish at all. His master went to look and when he came to the hiding place he found that there were indeed two sharpening-stones. Fan Wen then realised that there was something mysterious about the pair of carp. So he worked the stones, and from the metal he obtained from them forged two swords. Lifting the blades towards the Great Dyke (the mountains of the Annamite Chain) he cried: 'The carp are transformed into stones, the stones into swords by smelting. If there is power in them let the rock be split, the dyke be broken. If I succeed I shall become ruler of this kingdom. If the swords do not enter the rock, then they are without power.' As he then advanced, the swords split the Great Dyke, and the people, seeing this, adhered to him.

A Lohan or Arhat, one of the immediate disciples of Buddha and about to become a Bodhisattva. Under the influence of the saviour Kuan Yin, Lohans became increasingly identified with the Taoist Immortals. In his left hand the Lohan bears a dish of the peaches of mmortality. Reign of Khang Hsi. Musée Guimet.

Jade ring in the form of a dragon with a pearl held before its jaws. High-born travellers cast such rings into the Yellow River as a placatory offering to Ho Po, Count of the River before venturing to make the crossing. Though originally human sacrifices were made, Ho Po was said to be especially pleased with offerings of jade. British Museum.

The Thunderer, an ancient storm-deity, seen routing men and beasts with the sound of thunder, which he produces by beating drums with a hammer. His chariot is drawn by six boys. In later times, like Feng Po, he became an official in the Ministry of Thunder, and was called Lei Kung, Duke of Thunder. Rubbing of a stone relief from the tomb of the Wu family in Shantung. Han dynasty. National Gallery, Prague.

The sundered rock still exists, as do the swords, which have been handed down to his descendants from generation to generation.

Li hua lung, 'the carp becomes a dragon', is a phrase used to describe success in the public examinations. The carp became a dragon by passing through the Dragon Gate, the pass in the mountains which was cleft by Yu the Great. And to assassinate a prince who is hard of access, the dagger should be concealed within a fish.

KHUN-LUN

The cult of Thai Shan centred on a real mountain: the beliefs concerning Khun-lun to the far west relate to a mythical peak whose alleged location moved westwards in advance of each extension of geographical knowledge. It was to be identified with Sumeru, the axial mountain of Indian cosmic theories, once these became known to the Chinese, who seemed to find no incongruity in its peripheral situation. It was thought of as the source of the Yellow River and also, a manifest example of Indian influence, as the source of four rivers flowing to the four quarters. It was difficult of access, being encircled by water so thin that even a feather could not float upon it. (In another version the water was vermilion hued and flowed thrice about the mountain's foot: those who drank of it obtained immortality, for this realm of the far west was also a region where immortality could be won. It was the western counterpart of the floating paradises of the Eastern Sea.)

The mountain was vastly high, perhaps high enough to reach the sky itself, with a base which penetrated equally deeply into the earth. Khun-lun thus seems to have embodied both male and female principles. The triangle is the male organ as well as the mountain; the inverted triangle is female, but can it not also be the buried part of Khun-lun? The *mons veneris* is not simply the crest of the pubic bone, but the reverse mountain, the triangle with its apex pointing downwards.

Khun-lun was in nine stages (as was the sky), with doors on its sides or upon the summit itself from which the winds emerged. By the doors were wells of remarkably pure water.

Khun-lun was deemed to be the earthly home of the Lord of the Sky and was inhabited by varieties of mysterious beasts and deities. All were under the jurisdiction of a creature with human face, a tiger's body and limbs, and four tails. Goat-like creatures with four horns lived upon human flesh. A tiger-bodied creature with nine human heads guarded the door of light, which faced towards the east. The birds of the mountain executed the orders of the Lord of the Sky. As the Taoist canon developed and interest in the nature of Khun-lun increased it became more and more a paradise and its form was gradually conceived of in more architectural terms; but it never lost its role as a cosmic pillar.

THE LORD OF RAIN

The Lord of Rain was thought to dwell on its slopes. His dress was scale armour, yellow in colour: his headdress blue and yellow. In some stories he sprinkled water upon the earth from a watering-can; in others the sprinkler was a sword with which he drew water from a pot in his left hand. Another story tells how there was a fearful drought during the reign of Shen-nung, the last of the Three August Ones. Chhih Sung-tzu ordered a bottle of water to be poured into an earthenware bowl. Then he took a branch of a tree from the mountainside and dipped it into the bowl and sprinkled the earth. Clouds at once gathered and rain poured upon the earth until the rivers overflowed their banks. As a reward Chhih Sung-tzu was made Lord of Rain and went to dwell upon Khun-lun.

In another form he was conceived of as a silkworm chrysalis with a black-faced concubine who has a serpent in each hand and red and green serpents in her right and left ears. With him was a magic bird, *shang yang*, which had only one leg. Once it appeared at the court of the Prince of Chhi. Descending from the roof where it had perched, it entered the reception court, where it was observed to spread its wings and to dance upon its one leg. The prince sent an embassy to Lu to enquire from Confucius the

A fairy walking on the waves. Under the influence of Indian Buddhism much emphasis was placed on fairies, who inhabited mountains and water. They were often linked with the Immortals and imagined on every peak, but especially on Khun-lun. Painting after Chhien Hsuan of the Yuan dynasty (thirteenth century). British Museum.

76

Ploughing a ricefield with the aid of an ox. Mankind learnt the art of ploughing from the ox-headed mythical emperor Shen-nung; but the grains of rice were not filled until Kuan Yin took pity on the starving people, and men would have been unable to produce enough food if the plough-ox had not come down from Heaven to help them. Jade screen. Reign of Khang Hsi (1662-1722). Seattle Art Museum.

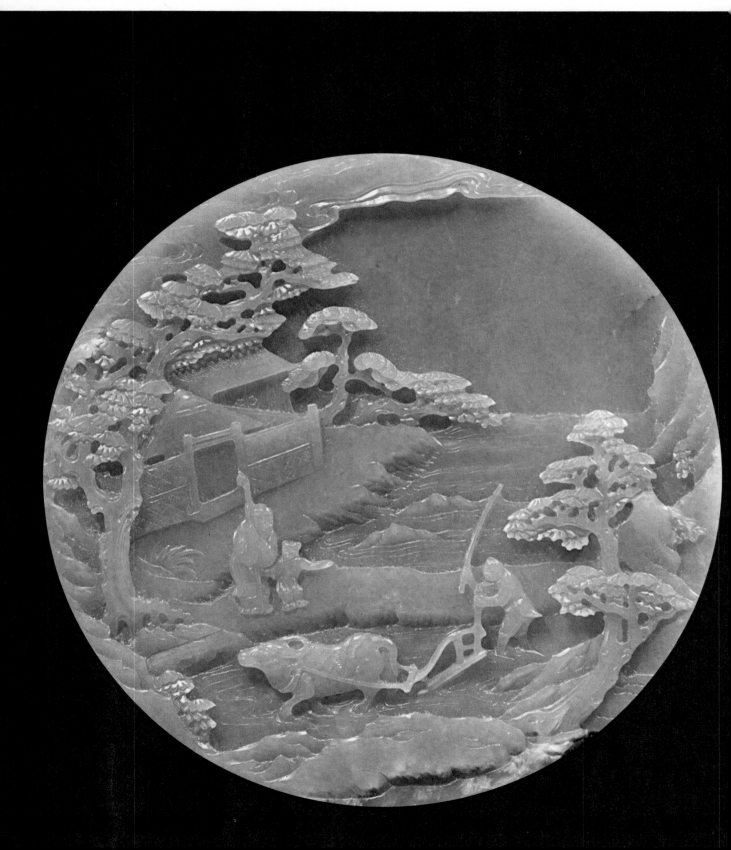

Jade screen illustrating the art of weaving silk. Sericulture was one of the basic arts of Chinese civilisation taught by the serpent-bodied Fu-hsi, the first of the mythical Three Sovereigns. The Heavenly Weaver-girl was the daughter of the sun-god. Jade screen. Reign of Khang Hsi (1662-1722). Seattle Art Museum.

Thai Shan, the mountain of the east from which the sun began its daily journey and to which in early times the souls of the dead were thought to return. The most important dynastic sacrifices were performed on its inaccessible peak. Landscape engraving from the *Ming-han ming-shan thu-pan hua-chi*. Ming dynasty. University of Hong Kong.

meaning of this apparition. The sage replied that the bird was a *shang yang* whose appearance foretold rain:

> In former times youths used to amuse themselves by hopping on one foot with hunched shoulders saying: it will rain because the *shang yang* is disporting himself, dancing to his own drum. Now that the bird is in Chhi, heavy rain will fall. The people must dig ditches and repair the dykes or all the land will be inundated.

The rains came, and only Chhi escaped damage, a fact which led the ruler of a neighbouring state to remark sadly on the fact that people seldom listened to the words of sages.

HSI WANG MU

Of all the deities connected with Khun-lun, the best known does not really seem to have belonged to the mountain in the beginning. This was Hsi Wang Mu, the Royal Mother of the Western Paradise. Her home was said, in the *Shan Hai Ching*, to be on a jade mountain to the north of Khun-lun and to the west of the Moving Sands. She was originally a fearful creature, with a human face, tiger's teeth and a leopard's tail, who dwelt in a cave in the mountain with her hair flowing round her as she sat on a stool. Three green birds (sometimes three-footed birds such as those that dwelt in the sun) brought her food. Her suzerainty was over plague and pestilence. How this monster became the beautiful goddess who presided over the Western Paradise is not at all clear, but in Taoist literature and folklore she is a beautiful and gracious being and guardian of the herb of immortality, the exact counterpart of Mu Kung, who presides over the East. (He is *yang*, she *yin*: from them, compound of primal vapour, Heaven and Earth are engendered with all beings that are found therein.)

Her palace is on Khun-lun, surrounded by a golden rampart and with a

magic fountain where the feast of the Immortals is held at the edge of the Lake of Gems. The meats include bear paws, monkey lips and dragon livers: the culmination of the repast is the service of the peaches from the magic tree. This is in leaf every three thousand years and its fruit takes another three thousand years to ripen. Then it is the birthday of Hsi Wang Mu and all the Immortals attend her birthday feast to eat the fruit which gives them their immortality. (It was this feast that Monkey stole in the famous story from the *Hsi yu chi*, p. 123.)

The Count of the River

All the rivers and streams of China had their deities and spirits, to whom offerings were made and about whom legends were recounted, but just as there was one river above all others, so there was one river-deity, Ho Po the Count of the River. Also known as Ping-i, he was the deity who controlled

the Yellow River and to whom official cult was paid and sacrifices and offerings made by the ruler. The Count was believed to have dedicated himself to the River by throwing himself in with a load of stones on his back: this act gave him magical power and gained him immortality.

The control of Ho-tsong, the Ancestral Village of the River, became an object of dynastic struggles: the river was the life of China. The rulers of Chhin called on the Count to witness their oaths, and when they gained control of Lin-tsin they presented girls of royal blood to be his bride. All those who crossed the great river made offerings, but it was those who lived on its banks and made their livings upon its waters who organised the great annual offerings. These were particularly centred at Lin-tsin and Ye.

Until the ending of the Chou dynasty the offerings included human sacrifices, each year seeing a girl offered to the

One of the three islands of the Immortals in the Eastern Sea. The inhabitants of this eastern paradise not only had the secret of immortality, but also the alchemical secrets of making gold. Men and animals on the islands were all coloured white, while all the buildings were made of silver and gold. Men could not approach the islands, for their ships were driven back by storms. Painting by Wang Chen. Sung dynasty. National Museum of Taiwan.

二第為此中卷四說王藏所府內

Kuan Yin, goddess of mercy, the female Chinese form of the Bodhisattva Avalokitesvara, who postponed her Buddhahood in order to help the people. Kuan Yin was particularly important in northern China. Red amber statuette. Wellcome Medical Museum.

The Seventh Hell, which was the place of punishment for desecrators of graves and eaters and sellers of human flesh. The Yama, King of the Seventh Hell, dressed like an emperor and surrounded by ministers or court officials, is receiving offerings from suppliants while he watches a dog and devils with flails chasing condemned souls into a river. Fourteenth-century painting.

Bronze *ting* decorated with hanging swords and cicadas, a vessel used for the preparation of sacrificial food and resembling the so-called tripod or cauldron of Yu, a symbol of dynastic power. The story of Kan Chiang and Mo Yeh illustrates the themes of sacrifice connected with cauldrons, swords and royal power. Shang or Early Chou. Minneapolis Institute of Arts.

Centre. The Black Warrior – tortoise and serpent – which symbolises the north. Unlike the other directions, the north was never worshipped in early times, and was feared as the nome of the destructive god of the ocean wind. But the Han ruled under the protection of water and of the North and sacrificed to the Black Emperor. White slip on earthenware. Northern Wei (A.D. 385-535). Seattle Art Museum.

Count as his bride. There was a college of sorcerers and sorceresses who managed the cult and the offerings and who chose the bride. The chosen girl was proclaimed a year in advance; then, when the season was right, she was taken in bridal finery to a pavilion on the river bank. After feasting and a ritual fast she was placed upon a marriage bed and this was launched into the flooding stream, where the Count claimed his bride.

The sacrifices at Ye were ended by Hsi-men Pao, an emissary of the Marquis Wen of Wei (427-387 B.C.), but those at Lin-tsin continued until the time of Shih Huang Ti. At Ye the emissary told

the chief sorceress that the girl was not sufficiently beautiful to be the Count's bride. He then instructed his soldiers to throw the chief sorceress into the river to explain to the Count why the bride was delayed. When she did not return, he had a second and then a third sorceress thrown in on the same mission. Then, reflecting that women would not know how to explain, he had the regional head thrown in too. After this all those still on the bank banged their foreheads upon the ground until the blood-flowed and their faces became ashen. Then the emissary stopped the ceremony, which was never resumed.

The Count of the River is capable of

wrath, but sacrifice to him is to obtain his support, not his forgiveness. The Chhu general Tseu-yu possessed a fine bonnet decorated with jade, which the deity coveted. He appeared therefore to the general in a dream and offered him victory over the prince of Chhin in return for the hat. The general failed to comply and was defeated at Chheng-pu on the banks of the Yellow River.

Sacrifices to Ho Po and his fellow river deities were one way of pleasing the waters, but there were other methods which could be used to deal with the great River. Then as now, the construction of dykes and dams and the cutting of canals were the methods recognised as most efficacious for flood-control and irrigation alike. And these skills were taught by Nu-kua, Kun and Yu, three of the principal characters in Chinese mythology.

These myths we shall consider in the next chapter, for they are part of the manner of life of the Chinese, for whom the flooding of their vast rivers is still a major problem. Here we may simply note that there is no question of the Flood in Chinese mythology being a universal punishment for human sin or wrong-doing. The rivers which overflow their banks are the source of a natural disaster that does not imply divine displeasure.

Yu-chhiang, god of the ocean wind, listening to the Doctrine. Painting by Chao Po-chu of the Sung dynasty; he belonged to the 'northern' school of painting, long associated with a sect of Zen Buddhism, and the subject shows a preoccupation with the new faith in relation to the old deity. National Museum of Taiwan.

The useful arts

Yu, master of floods, who by working continuously for thirteen years at his great task of flood control earned a high reputation for selfless devotion to duty, and became emperor in succession to Shun. Yu founded the Hsia dynasty despite his own wishes: the people ignored his nomination of his minister to succeed him and installed his son Chhi on the throne. Yu was thus the first king to be succeeded by his son. Painting by Ma Lin. Sung dynasty. National Museum of Taiwan.

In the most ancient past, when men were few and animals many, human beings could not defend themselves against birds, beasts, insects or reptiles. A sage appeared at that time who made wooden nests to protect men from harm. The delighted people made him ruler of the world, calling him the Nest Builder. They lived on fruits, berries, mussels and clams, stinking and evil-smelling things which hurt their intestines so that they fell ill in large numbers. Then another sage appeared who used a fire-drill to produce fire which transformed the putrid, stinking food. The delighted people made him ruler of the world under the name of Drill Man.

'In the less remote past there was a great flood in the world, but Kun and Yu of the Hsia dynasty opened up channels to control the water . . . When Yao ruled the world his roof thatch was untrimmed and men did not plant speckled beans. He ate coarse millet and bitter green soup; his winter dress was deerskin, while for summer he wore rough fibres. Even a lowly gatekeeper was no worse clothed and provided for than he. When Yu ruled the world, he led his people with plough and spade, working until there was no further down on his thighs or hair upon his shins . . . In the time of Shun, the Miao tribes were unsubmissive and Yu proposed to attack them. Shun said: "It will not do, for to take up arms while the ruler's virtue is unperfected would be a violation of the Way". Then Shun taught good government for three years. After this he took up shield and battle

axe and performed the war dance, whereupon Miao submitted. But in the war with the Kungkung tribe men used iron lances with steel points that reached as far as the enemy, so that a man without stout helmet and armour was likely to be wounded.'

Such is the account which Han Fei Tzu gives of the early stages of Chinese cultural history. Other accounts tell of the inventions and discoveries assigned to the various rulers and sovereigns in pre-Hsia times, or to their ministers. The most extensive set of stories is that which deals with the control of floods and the development of irrigation which, in legend, began with the moment when Kung Kung, defeated in his attempt to wrest sovereignty of the world from Yao, overturned Mount

Pu Chou, tilting the earth and causing the rivers to flood. But this is only one of a number of flood stories, so that we find many confusions in the surviving textual versions of the myths and legends. Some of these we may now consider.

Nu-kua and Fu-hsi

We have already met the goddess Nu-kua as a creator of mankind. But her services as restorer of order to the world after Kung Kung's attack on Mount Pu Chou are equally important in the cycle of stories about her, even though it does not seem that the original version of the legend was about Kung Kung at all. It may well have concerned a quite other monster who became assimilated to him when scholars tried to produce

Centre. The serpent-bodied sovereign Fu-hsi, who taught men how to fish, to domesticate animals, and to breed silkworms, and to whom the first dragon appeared in 2962 B.C. He invented trigrams, the basis of writing and scholarship, as well as music and the instrument with which Yu measured, and so encompassed, the universe. Painting on silk of the Chhien Lung period (1736-95). Metropolitan Museum of Art, New York.

Yao, fourth of the Five Emperors. He was famed for his benign rule. With the help of Yi the Divine Archer he subdued the unruly winds and with the help of Khun he attempted to quell the floodwaters of the Yellow River. When Yao resolved to pass his throne to Shun rather than to his own son the ten suns appeared together and nearly destroyed the world. Painting on silk of the Chhien Lung period, (1736-95). Metropolitan Museum of Art, New York.

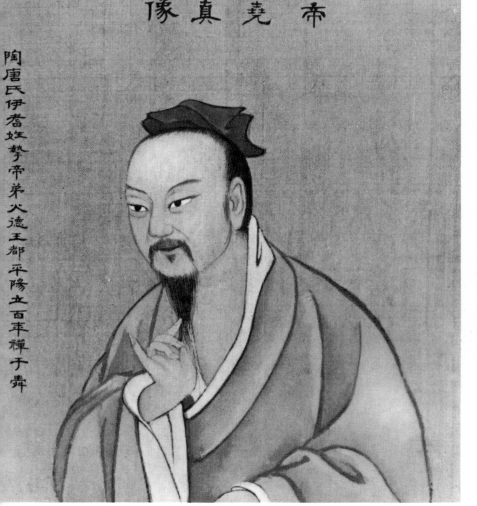

The attempt by Chhin Shih Huang Ti, first unifier of China, to have one of the Nine Cauldrons of Yu hauled out of the Ssu river. Possession of the cauldrons, like sacrifice on Thai Shan, would confirm the founder of the new dynasty as Son of Heaven; but every time the cauldron reached the surface a dragon bit through the ropes, and the cauldron was lost for ever. Rubbing from a stone relief in the tomb of the Wu family in Shantung. Second century A.D.

Rubbing from a stone relief in the tomb of the Wu family in Shantung showing two calendar plants, the invention of Fu-hsi. The tree on the right grew one leaf every day for fifteen days after which it lost one leaf a day; it thus measured the days of the month. The other tree grew a leaf every month for six months and then lost them one by one, thus marking the months of the year. Han dynasty.

some version to reconcile traditions of different ethnic and cultural groups during China's formative period.

In early sources Nu-kua occurs alone, but later she is always associated with Fu-hsi, who, in the traditional account of pre-dynastic China, is the first of the Three Sovereigns preceding the Five Emperors. She is either his younger sister, or, once she has invented marriage, his wife. The conflict between her role as sister and wife is, however, by no means absolute, for in the myths of non-Chinese tribes in the south we find that it is from the incestuous intercourse of brother and sister that a new race of men is created after a destructive flood has eliminated mankind. As a pair, Fu-hsi and Nu-kua are first represented in Han times as beings with human bodies and dragon tails, which are intertwined to link them. Fu-hsi carries a set-square, Nu-kua compasses: the latter are round, sky, while the former is square, earth. Once again we are in the presence of the male-female, *yin-yang* system. Together compasses *kuei* and set-square *chu* symbolise *kuei-chu*: order, proper conduct. To restore the devastation caused by Kung Kung's violence is to re-establish pattern in the world.

In the *Lieh Tzu* the account of Nu-Kua's achievement reads thus: In oldest times the four cardinal points were out of place; the Nine Provinces lay open; the sky did not wholly cover the earth; the earth did not wholly support the sky; fire burnt ceaselessly without dying out; the waters flowed on without ceasing; wild beasts devoured the peaceful people; birds of prey carried off the aged and children. Then Nu-kua smelted the stones of five colours to make good the azure sky; she cut off the feet of a tortoise to fix the cardinal points; she slew the black dragon to save the country of Chhi; she piled up ashes of reeds to stop the overflowing waters. All was tranquil at that time; everything was at peace.

This summary account of the activities of the goddess is full of difficulties, but one thing is clear: her task is to restore order. In another text the waters are described as licentious and needing to be brought back into a system of equilibrium. The reference to fire which burns ceaselessly while the waters overflow may relate to another part of the story of Kung Kung, where the Spirit of Fire, Chu-jung, was sent to punish the monster but failed in his task. (As we shall see later, however, the Fire Spirit was called in to punish another hero figure who tried to stop flooding.) The islands of the Eastern Sea rested upon tortoises, though these had feet. It may be that the concept of stability, embodied in the tortoise, which here requires cardinal pillars, can only be

A winged dragon. This was the form in which Yu was born. The winged dragon aided Huang Ti in his struggle against the rebel Chhih-yu, son of Shen-nung, and on Huang Ti's instructions became the instrument with which Yu cut ditches to channel the floodwaters. Probably the handle of a vessel. Sixth-fifth centuries B.C. British Museum.

expressed by the use of a tortoise part, the leg, for the whole. The commentators say that the ash of reeds is efficacious in the repair of breached dykes because reeds grow in water. It may be that the concept of reed (water) and ash (fire) is also seen as an expression of harmonious union *yin-yang*, of order and equilibrium. Such an idea is certainly hidden in the reference to the stones of five colours, for these appear in a number of texts, often relating to the forging of magic swords or cauldrons whose power depends upon the combination of the five ores in a proper and harmonious alloy. The black dragon which here threatens Chhi, an allusion that seems to belong to another story, is a rain demon, whose fault is presumably excess of zeal. Some commentators have claimed that the black dragon is Kung Kung, but there is no reason to think that this is so.

Yao and Khun

There is another flood legend which is considerably more circumstantial and which contains the history of the origins of hydraulic engineering. This is set in the time of the emperor Yao, when the overflowing waters reached up to the sky. Yao sought the advice of Four-Mountains, who bade him ask the help of Khun, the great grandson of Huang Ti, who is sometimes described as having the form of a white horse. Yao was reluctant to do so, but in the end agreed. Khun set about his task by building dams, but these collapsed under the weight of the waters before they were strong enough to confine

them. A tortoise, some say it was three-footed, and a horned owl appeared, and advised Khun to steal the Swelling Earth from Huang Ti. This alone could block the waters and confine them in seemly manner. Khun took their counsel and stole the magic earth which had the property of growing ceaselessly. With its aid he began to control the waters and thus incurred the wrath of Huang Ti. The latter sent Chu-jung, Spirit of Fire and heavenly executioner, to dispose of Khun, as he had once been sent to punish Kung Kung for causing a flood. Chu-jung slew Khun on Feather Mountain. This punishment took place in the sixty-ninth year of Yao's reign, after Khun had toiled for nine years. Some say that Khun was torn to pieces by tortoises and owls, but in fact his body lay as it was in life and did not decompose. Finally, after three years, his belly was slashed open with the sword of Wu and there emerged his son Yu in the form of a winged and horned dragon. Khun turned into a yellow bear and threw himself into the river, though there are accounts which say he became a three-footed tortoise or a yellow dragon.

Yu, master of floods

Yu, learning from his father's misfortune, went to see Huang Ti in Heaven and obtained from him permission to use the Swelling Earth. He was thus equipped to accept the invitation of Shun, who had succeeded Yao some two years earlier, to control the floods. In some accounts Huang Ti gave to Yu as much Swelling Earth as could be

The ox-headed divine farmer Shen-nung, second of the Three Sovereigns, who taught men the arts of agriculture as well as the use of herbal drugs. He was also god of the burning wind, and during his reign the people were saved from drought only by the intervention of Chhih Sung-tzu, who became the Lord of Rain, and who later sided with Shen-nung's son against Huang Ti. Engraving from *San-tsai thu-hui* (1607 edition). University of Hong Kong.

piled on to the back of a black tortoise and also ordered the Winged Dragon, who had aided him in his struggle against the monster Chhih-yu, to assist him. Yu began his task by damming the springs from which the waters came: there were 233,559 of these, but with the Swelling Earth he could block them all. Then he built mountains at the corners of the earth to ensure that there would be regions that could not be submerged. They also served to anchor what was otherwise in danger of being swept away by the floods. Of course, there were inevitably small openings which escaped even Yu's thorough labours and it is because of these that there are still floods. The mountains nevertheless ensure that the floods are never so engulfing as in the time before Yu began his task. There still remained the problem of the water already on the earth. With the tail of the Winged Dragon Yu now cut ditches by which the water was guided back into the river beds, whence it flowed to the sea; but sometimes mere ditches were not enough and Yu had to tunnel through mountains or split them in order to make a passage for the great waters on their journey to the sea.

After Yu had toiled for thirty years he had reached the age when, according to Confucian tradition, it was proper to take a wife. One day, as he thought of this, he approached a clump of willows from which he saw a white fox with nine tails appear. This reminded him of a prophecy that to see such a beast was to guarantee sovereignty, while to marry the girl of Thu Shan was to obtain a flourishing lineage. He made his way to Mount Thu, where he found a girl waiting for him: her name was Nu-chiao. They were married and Nu-chiao accompanied Yu in his work. One day he was engaged in tunnelling through a mountain, a task which he carried out by transforming himself into a bear. Now it was his custom, when he was ready for his food, to summon Nu-chiao by beating upon a drum: on this day he fell against a stone which sounded like the drum. His wife hurried to him and saw a

great bear from whom she fled in terror. As she ran in panic Yu pursued her, still in the form of a bear. Slowly he overtook her, but as he was on the point of reaching her, she turned into a rock. Now Yu knew that she was pregnant and as she underwent this transformation, he begged her to leave him their child. But the embryo remained within the rock until the full term of nine months. Then the rock split and a boy Chhi, 'Split', was born.

It was Chhi who in succeeding his father as ruler of Hsia established for the first time in China the rule of primogeniture. According to Ssu-ma Chhien, Yu had nominated his minister Po-yi as his successor but the feudal lords deserted him and came to support Chhi, saying that their prince was the son of the sovereign Yu. In another tradition Chhi is said to have slain Po-yi and seized power: there may be in this some recollection of an older system whereby a minister exercised power during the period of mourning between one ruler and the next, a three-year interregnum after which the minister was supposed to instal a legitimate successor to exercise full suzerainty. Chhi rode upon two dragons, who were able to transport him on visits to Heaven. There he heard divine music and it was by this means that men learnt to compose music.

Although he had lost his wife in this dramatic fashion, Yu's work was not yet complete. There were still monsters to be slain and works to be accomplished. He fought against a vassal of Kung Kung called Hsiang-yao, a serpent-bodied creature with nine heads, whose pastureland was nine mountains and whose vomit formed evil springs and marshes. When Yu slew him, his foul blood corrupted the fields and the crops would not grow. Where his body lay there was so great a flood that the land was uninhabitable. Yu tried to clear up the mess by containing it within a dyke (as his predecessor had tried unsuccessfully to control Kung Kung's flood by embankments). Thrice he built the walls and thrice they were breached. Then he dug a lake and was successful. In the middle of this lake Yu built a tower, some say with the earth from the excavations for the lake. This set a pattern for later times when the erection of a tower was held to be efficacious for the control of dragons.

It is probably in his capacity as the master of floods that Yu is said to have received from the Count of the River a river map which, it is sometimes said, was placed on the back of a horse. The gift is sometimes made to Fu-hsi, the inventor of trigrams – which were, in fact, the symbols employed on the map. Yu and Fu-hsi are linked in various ways, for according to another story, Yu, while engaged in his channelling of the waters, penetrated a deep cavern in whose interior he discovered Fu-hsi with his human face and serpent body. The latter presented Yu with a jade slab fashioned into a scale for measuring Heaven and Earth. This refers to another of Yu's functions, for he traversed all the earth and its waters, measuring them and determining the directions and distances. Thus in one version it seems to be implied that he was responsible for the construction of the cardinal mountains. In the chapter of the *Shu Ching* known as the Tribute of Yu there are accounts of Yu's supposed activities in delineating the empire and its peoples and products. In these descriptions the real and the mythical are apparently given the same credence. The text presumably dates from the fifth century B.C., but represents a much older tradition. It is interesting to note that since Yu has to travel to carry out the task of describing the land he is also credited with the invention of various means of transport. In this system the earth is square: the distance between each of the cardinal poles 233,575 paces, the figures having been established either by Yu himself or by his two assistants, Ta-chang and Shou-hai.

The knowledge of the earth's geography was translated by Yu into a tangible record which became the palladium of the Hsia, the so-called Nine Cauldrons. Traditionally these were cast by Yu himself from metal brought from far-off countries by the Nine Shepherds. It appears that each cauldron bore repre-

Yu, son of Khun, the third of the Five Emperors who brought the arts of civilisation to the Chinese people. In the service of the fifth Emperor, Shun, Yu mastered the elements of water and of metal, controlling floods and becoming a smith. He mapped out the universe and finally claimed the throne as founder of the Hsia dynasty. Engraving from *San-tsai thu-hui* (1607 edition). University of Hong Kong.

Nu-kua (left) holding compasses and Fu-hsi, holding a set-square. By inventing marriage and a *yin-yang* partnership with Fu-hsi, Nu-kua re-established cosmic equilibrium after Kung Kung's destructive attack. Below is Hsi Wang Mu with two servants pounding the herb of immortality. All are winged as an indication of immortality. Pillar of a tomb at Pei Chai Ts'un.

Chu-jung, Spirit of Fire and heavenly executioner, who was alternatively the third son of the deity of Thai Shan, or the son of one of the mythical emperors, who instructed him to keep order on earth. He killed both Kung Kung, for bringing floods, and Khun, for stealing the means to control the same floods. He was especially honoured by the emperors of the tenth and eleventh centuries. Victoria and Albert Museum.

sentations of provincial symbols and thus subsumed all the beings, and products, of the region in question, together with some kind of map. The cauldrons were cast when the Hsia dynasty was at its most powerful. As the power of the dynasty declined, so the weight of the cauldrons decreased. They could thus be more easily borne off or even transport themselves, a capacity which they owed to the Female Tortoise of the North, whose head faced to the right and who had been consulted on the occasion of their being cast. The whole of the tradition regarding the cauldrons seems to link Yu with clans of miners, the possible connection being through the mountains: here Yu had dug passes

for the easier dispersal of the waters just as the miners dug their galleries for ores. Each dynasty possessed cauldrons of this type and similar vessels were to be found in the contiguous regions under Chinese influence. Those of the Nguyen dynasty still survive at their capital Hue in central Vietnam.

In his capacity as caster of the Nine Cauldrons, Yu the Great was a smith. Now Granet has shown, in masterly fashion, how important in the cultural history of China were confraternities of craftsmen, mainly smiths, which seem to have grown out of groups of husbandmen who developed specialist skills. And it was in such fraternities that agricultural techniques appear to have developed.

Shen-nung

The successor to Nu-kua, the ox-headed Shen-nung, is said to have invented the plough and to have taught men basic agriculture, but it seems likely that he was first and foremost god of the burning wind, of the technique of clearing scrub jungle by fire in order to set seeds in the area, rich in potash, which remains after the fire has passed. If this is so, then one can understand that, as planting succeeds to gathering and ploughing to slash-and-burn, the new inventions called for by new techniques will be attributed to the originally presiding deity.

Huang Ti and Chhih-yu

Shen-nung's son, minister or grandson – the texts are wonderfully confused – was called Chhih-yu. Like Shen-nung, he was ox-headed, with sharp horns, a bronze forehead and iron skull. His temples were covered with hair which bristled like swords. He was the inventor of war and of weapons, and fought against Huang Ti (either the Yellow Emperor or the August Sovereign: the texts are ambiguous and reflect the confusion of innumerable conflations). The struggle between Huang Ti and Chhih-yu is a classic example of the struggle between ruler and rebel (who is often a minister in revolt). Both sides had the aid of celestial creatures: the Winged

Huang Ti, the Yellow Emperor, first of the Five Emperors, who was credited with the invention of the chariot wheel and potter's wheel as well as that of the compass. When his rebel minister Chhih-yu invented war and weapons Huang Ti resisted him with these inventions and with ships and armour, which he introduced to mankind. From *Li-tai ku-jen hsiang-tsan* (1498 edition). University of Hong Kong.

Dragon sided with Huang Ti; the Count of the Wind and the Master of Rain with Chhih-yu. When Chhih-yu called down thick fog to confuse the fighting, Huang Ti invented the compass so as to guide his own forces. The horns upon which his troops blew made the sound of dragons. Ultimately Huang Ti summoned from Heaven the goddess Pa, who, in the eyes of some, was his daughter, and bade her drive off the rain and wind. Being drought, she was able to do so. Chhih-yu was defeated and beheaded, but Pa the goddess of drought stayed upon earth, for reasons which are not clear, and that is why drought still inflicts itself upon mankind. Despite her previous assistance to him, Huang Ti was forced in the end to send her into exile so that humanity might survive.

This series of tales illustrates an important conceptual pattern for the transfer of power from one dynasty to the next: Chhih-yu is the son of Shen-nung and a minister; Huang Ti must overcome him in order that he may succeed to the throne as the first of the Five Emperors. Both are leaders of confraternities represented by their acolytes: Drought and Rain Dragon, Wind and Rain. But in the time before Huang Ti the basic elements of Chinese existence had been expounded to mankind: the floods controlled, the earth measured and mapped, and the plough and agriculture made available.

Ploughing scene with two of the Eight Immortals. Originally oxen existed only in Heaven, but owing to a mistake of the Ox star the Emperor of Heaven decreed that they should remain on Earth and help men with their ploughing. They were regarded as beneficent creatures who performed many services to mankind despite maltreatment. c. eighteenth-nineteenth centuries A.D. Jade carving.

Peasant myths

Side by side with these formal myths, reflecting no doubt scholarly politickings in support of factional interests, we find popular tales which give accounts of specific discoveries in the realm of agriculture and the like. Such stories represent a tradition that the scholars either overlooked or thought unworthy of their attention.

The ox, helper of farmers

In general, the popular tales are not concerned with cosmogonies or with attempts to construct cosmologies. If they deal with origins, it is with the origin of useful things, as we shall observe. Sometimes they are tinged with elements from one or other of the faiths which have from time to time spread through China. A good example of this is to be seen in the versions of the story of the way in which mankind was provided with plough-oxen.

In the past men had to struggle for food. Despite the fact that they worked day and night, it was only on every third or fourth day, sometimes even less frequently, that they were able to eat. This state of affairs distressed the Emperor of Heaven, who sent down the Ox star from the sky to tell men that if they were to work hard and diligently, then they would always be able to eat every third day. But the Ox was stupid: he went hastily down to Earth and told men that the Emperor of Heaven had decreed that they should eat three times a day. Since the Ox had made a mistake in his instructions, he was sent back to earth to help men with their ploughing, for with only their own hands and feet it would not have been possible for men to prepare sufficient food. That is why plough-oxen, which originally were to be found only in Heaven, exist on Earth.

In a Buddhist version of the story Ti-tsang Buddha, Ksitigarbha Bodhisattva, who is believed to rule over Hell, was aroused to compassion by man's struggle for food. This story also explains why the Bodhisattva is ruler of Hell and indicates how Buddhist deities are subordinate to 'native' Chinese ones. The Bodhisattva suggested to the Jade Emperor that the heavenly Ox should be sent down to earth to aid men in the preparation of the fields. But the Jade Emperor would not agree for he knew that while men would care for the ox so long as it was able to pull the plough, once it was too feeble they would kill it, eat its flesh and tan its hide. This the Bodhisattva disputed. He pledged that if such a thing were to happen, he would suffer banishment to Hell. Of course things turned out as the Jade Emperor had feared: as soon as the ox was too feeble to pull the plough, its flesh was eaten, its hide stripped off and used. And though the ox pleaded with its ungrateful users, they remained unmoved. Then the Jade Emperor was wroth and banished Ti-tsang Phusa to Hell, where as an additional punishment he had to keep his eyes closed except on the thirtieth day of the seventh month. And so it is that on that day men light candles and burn incense in his honour.

The origins of crops

We have already seen that agriculture and its techniques were the invention of the pre-Yin rulers of China, at least so far as the formal myths are concerned. There are many different stories, however, about the origins of specific plants and the like.

THE INTRODUCTION OF RICE
According to one of these the rice plant existed from the beginning but its ears were not filled. This was the time when men lived by hunting and gathering. The goddess Kuan Yin saw that men lived in hardship and near starvation. She was moved to pity and resolved to help them. She went secretly into the ricefields and squeezed her breasts so that the milk flowed into the ears of the rice plants. Almost all of them were filled, but to complete her task she had

to press so hard that a mixture of milk and blood flowed into the plants. That is why there are two kinds of rice, the white from the milk, the red from the mixture of milk and blood.

In another story rice is the gift of a dog. After the floods had been controlled by Yu, men found that all the old plants had been destroyed, but that no new ones had taken their place. So they had to live by hunting. One day a dog was seen to emerge from a waterlogged field. From its tail there hung bunches of long yellow ears full of seeds, which people planted in the wet, but drained fields. The seeds grew and the plants ripened to give the people rice. For this they were very grateful to the dog, so before eating they always offered a little food to the dog and at the first meal after the rice-harvest the food was shared with the dog.

THE *LO-PHU* RADISH
Sometimes stories of this kind are also edifying moralities, such as one from central China which tells of the origin of the red-cored radish, *lo-phu*. This relates how Mu-lien, a good and virtuous man, suffered on account of his mother, a lazy scold who killed many animals to eat. When Mu-lien reproached his mother for taking life, she cursed him, an act which caused him much grief. One day Mu-lien's mother fell ill and knew that she was going to die. She told her son that as a punishment for having put to death so many living things, she knew that her soul would be banished to Hell for ever. On her death her dutiful son spent all his fortune on priests to recite prayers to save his mother from Hell. When the money was finished he became a monk and devoted himself to the same cause. By his merit and virtue he became a Buddha and was then able to descend into Hell to rescue his mother. He seized her in his arms and ran with her until, exhausted by his efforts, he was forced to lie down by the side of a field. His mother, whose punishment in Hell had

Tsai Shen, god of wealth, universally worshipped but especially by poor peasants. He lived on earth as a hermit whose miraculous powers included the ability to ride on the black tiger shown here. He fought for Wu, founder of the Chou dynasty, against the last of the Shang, Chou Hsin. He was killed by sorcery, but was later immortalised as god of riches. Gilt wood figure. Horniman Museum.

The Five Buddhas. Though formally subordinate to the native Chinese religions, Buddhism captured the popular imagination and was assimilated to some of the oldest Chinese beliefs. Thus the Five Buddhas correspond to the Great Emperors of the Five Peaks and are thus associated with the Taoist symbolism of the five elements. c. late seventeenth century A.D. Buddhist scroll painting.

The goddess Kuan Yin, enthroned on a lotus rising from the waters. She was the Chinese form of the Bodhisattva Avalokitesvara, who by the Thang dynasty had become a female goddess of mercy and bringer of children, identified with an ancient Chinese mother-goddess. Her milk, compassionately given to mankind, filled the ears of the rice plant. Eighteenth-century scroll painting Wellcome Medical Museum.

included starvation, saw that there were radishes in the field and, pulling one up, ate it. Mu-lien was appalled, for if the deity of Heaven noticed the theft it would lead to his mother's return to Hell for all eternity. So he cut off his finger and pushed it into the hole left by the stolen vegetable, where it grew as a red-cored radish. Mu-lien, who thus exemplified the virtue of filial piety, was the Buddhist teacher Maudgalyayana, whose personal name in folk-mythology is Lo Pu, a fact which probably explains why he is credited with the origin of the *lo-phu* radish.

THE CREATION OF OPIUM

An interesting story occurs in various forms to account for the origins of opium, tobacco or betel. The story tells of a man with a very ugly wife who upset him so that he could do nothing but curse her and threaten to throw her out. The wife accepted his ill-treatment, for she loved him dearly; but finally she fell ill of despair. As the hour of her death approached she said to her husband that despite the evil way in which he had treated her, he would realise after her death how much she loved him. About a week after her burial the husband learnt that a beautiful white flower had appeared on her grave. Within the flower was a small round fruit. This curious phenomenon worried the widower, who remembered the dying woman's words and began to regret his ill-behaviour. He wondered whether she had turned into a plant in order to injure him. Finally thoughts of his dead wife so filled his mind that he could neither sleep nor work. He fell ill, but he had no children to care for him, nor could the doctors help him. Then one night his wife appeared to him in a dream. She told him that the plant on her grave was formed from her soul: from a cut in the central fruit a juice would appear which, once it had hardened, could be smoked in a pipe. If her husband smoked the juice every day he would be relieved of his suffering. In the morning he did just this and with the first pipeful his suffering was eased. Thus the wife redeemed her dying pledge to prove her love.

THE DISCOVERY OF SALT

Another story deals with the discovery of salt, a commodity not only valued for itself but also of great importance in the imperial revenue system. One day a poor peasant working in fields by the seashore saw a phoenix perched on a mound on the edge of the sea. As he knew that there was always treasure buried where a phoenix perched, as soon as the bird flew away he began to dig on the spot. He found nothing but some curious earth and concluded that it must be of value. He took it home with him hoping to make his fortune with it; but then he reflected that to fail to report finding treasure to the emperor was to incur the death penalty. Obviously he could not risk marketing his find. He decided therefore to report his discovery at court. He duly presented himself before the emperor and told of the circumstances which led to his appearing with the rather unpleasantly smelling clod of earth. The emperor was not pleased and, accusing the wretched man of wasting his imperial time, ordered his immediate execution.

The piece of earth was forgotten on a shelf. But it was the wet season and one day as the cook was passing by with a dish for the emperor's meal a drop from the moist clod fell into the food. There was no time to prepare another dish, so the cook placed the contaminated one before his master. The latter at the first taste recognised that the food was incomparably finer than any he had tasted before and demanded an explanation from the cook. He, not daring to dissemble, had to admit that there had been an accident between kitchen and table. The emperor, wondering whether after all the peasant's discovery was of value, sampled the juice that ran from the clod of earth on his food. There was no doubt: the flavours were immeasurably enhanced. Then orders were given for the mound to be exploited and it was found that the earth could be moistened and then dried to produce white, flavour-enhancing crystals. Nothing could be done for the peasant, but his son was appointed to a high post and grew rich.

The pumpkin girl and the Great Wall

Among the many folktales collected by Lin Lan, there can be little doubt that the best known is that of Meng Chiang Nu. Its widespread popularity is the result of its frequent use in theatrical pieces from the time of the Ming dynasty onwards, but the story is very much older. Indeed, as Ku Chieh-kang has shown, the original story goes back to pre-Han times: when the theme was made to centre about the construction of the Great Wall of China, completed by Chhin Shih Huang Ti in the third century B.C., the form of the story was already well established, with its emphasis on loyalty and adherence to a husband in disgrace. In the form recorded by Lin Lan, the story combines a number of motifs from different sources and provides a good example of an evolved Chinese folkstory.

The land of the Meng family was separated from that of the Chiang by a wall. In one year the two families each

The three gods of happiness crossing the seas to their Palace of Immortality in the Happy Isles. They are Shou-lao, god of long life, Fu-hsing, god of happiness, and Lu-hsing, god of salaries or of functionaries. All lived on earth as men and by good fortune or merit were deified – which in part explains their popularity. Hsi Wang Mu and an attendant follow them. Porcelain dish. Reign of Yung Cheng (1723-35). Victoria and Albert Museum.

planted a climbing pumpkin by the wall and when the plants grew they met at the wall top and joined together. From this union an enormous fruit grew. When it had ripened it was gathered by the two families together, for after much discussion as to the ownership of the plant, it had been agreed that each family should have a half of the fruit. When it was divided, however, they found inside a beautiful little girl. They agreed to bring her up jointly and called her Meng Chiang, from the names of the two foster families.

This was in the time when Shih Huang Ti of the Chhin dynasty, fearful of Hunnish threats against the empire had resolved to build a wall along the northern frontier of China. But as soon as a section of the wall was completed it collapsed. Finally a sage advised the emperor that it was necessary to immure a living human victim at each mile of the wall's ten thousand mile length. The emperor adopted his advice and the empire lived in terror as the demand for victims grew. Then another scholar went to the emperor and suggested a method that would provide the necessary number of offerings without imposing further terror on the people. What was needed was to sacrifice a man called Wan, for since the name Wan meant 'ten thousand', his sacrifice would meet the requirements of the spirits which were destroying the wall as it was built. The delighted emperor sent at once for Wan, but the latter had heard of the proposal for his becoming an offering and had fled. Now it so happened that he was hiding in a tree in the garden of Meng Chiang's house, when she went out by moonlight to bathe in the pool there. In her pleasure she said, 'If any man were to see me now, as I am naked, then I would happily belong to him for ever.' And Wan called out from his tree, 'I have seen you.' So Meng Chiang and he were married. In the course of their wedding feast, soldiers came and seized Wan, leaving his bride in tears and the marriage unconsummated.

Though Meng Chiang had never known her husband, she was as bound to him in memory as any other wife would have been, and she undertook a perilous journey to the Great Wall in search of her husband's bones. But when she reached the wall she was appalled at its length, and did not know where she should begin her search. As she sat and wept, the wall took pity on her and collapsed to reveal the remains of her husband.

Now when the emperor heard of Meng Chiang's devoted search, he wished to see her; and when he did so he was so struck by her beauty that he determined to make her his empress. When Meng Chiang learned of this inescapable decision she agreed, subject to three conditions: there should be a forty-nine day funerary feast in honour of her husband; the emperor and the high officials of the court should attend the ceremonies; and an altar forty-nine feet high should be erected by the riverbank where she might make offerings to her dead husband. If these conditions were met, then she would marry the emperor. Chhin Shih Huang Ti consented without demur.

When all had been made ready as Meng Chiang had required, she mounted upon the high altar in the presence of the emperor and his court, and began to revile him for all his cruelty and evil. But the emperor took no action. Then she threw herself from the altar into the river. At this the emperor could restrain himself no longer, but bade his soldiers drag her from the water, cut her body into pieces, and grind her bones to dust. And when they did so, the pieces turned into little silver-coloured fish in which the soul of the faithful Meng Chiang continues to live.

Tshai the brickmaker

The theme of human sacrifice in order to bring about the completion of a piece of work is by no means uncommon in Chinese myths and legends. Eberhard records an interesting story from Chekiang in which such an event is related about brickmaking. It is uncertain how late into historical times such sacrifices actually took place, but

The Great Wall of China, erected by Shih Huang Ti of the Chhin dynasty as a protection against attack by the Huns in the north. The large-scale expenditure of resources, the conscription of labour, and the loss of life caused by the rapid building of this vast wall across rugged terrain gave rise to the myth of Meng Chiang Nu, the Pumpkin Girl.

98

Brass handle in the shape of a dragon-headed
door-guardian. Dragons were normally beneficent
but in some forms, like the *thao-thieh*, could be
frightening. From a Mongolian temple door. Religious Museum. Ulan Bator, Mongolia.

Red lacquer panel with the *pa kua* symbols. In the
centre are the interlocked *yin* and *yang* symbols, the
opposing and complementary principles of the
universe. They are surrounded by the Eight Trigrams, the mystic symbols which were the key
to knowledge and the basis of calligraphy. Wellcome
Medical Museum.

Detail of an emperor's marriage robe, showing the five-clawed imperial *lung* (dragon), a rain-spirit which symbolised the emperor himself, and three of the twelve imperial symbols: above, the constellations, to which the emperor made offerings at the Altar of Heaven; left, the *fu* symbol of happiness; right, the axe symbolising the power to punish. Nineteenth century. Victoria and Albert Museum.

we have already noted the frequent occurrence of human sacrifices in Shang times, both in funerary contexts and in connection with important buildings. The Chekiang story seems to belong to a stage at which the shift from human to animal sacrifices had already taken place.

There was once a village of brick-makers. The villagers were generally prosperous and careful to maintain good relations with the god of the brick-kilns. Whenever a new kiln was brought into use, a pig and a sheep were sacrificed in front of the furnace door in honour of the deity. To omit the offering was to risk the production of soft, yellow bricks which could not find a market, or even the collapse of the whole kiln. Now though the villagers lived on good terms with one another, there was one man, Tshai, who was determined to acquire control of the whole business of the village. To do this he built a vast new kiln some few miles away, but when it came to be fired the out-turn of bricks was quite useless: all were soft and yellow. Neither the builders of the kiln nor his own workmen could suggest any reason for this, but finally one old man suggested that a fortune-teller should be consulted. This was agreed and an answer obtained. It appeared that the traditional sacrifices were insufficient in Tshai's case, because of his evil heart. The god of the kiln would be satisfied with nothing less than the sacrifice of the would-be monopolist's daughter.

Tshai went at once to a far off village and there bought a thirteen-year-old girl as a substitute for his own daughter, a girl of the same age who was at the time living with the family into which she was in due course to marry. Tshai brought back his true daughter and the girl he had purchased – they were strikingly alike – and lodged them together until the time of the sacrificial feast. In order that the bought girl should not learn of her true destiny, Tshai ordered her to eat and to sleep with his daughter on the eve of the sacrifice. Few knew of Tshai's intentions, but he instructed some of his workmen that when the girl arrived in the morning with their breakfast they should cast her alive into the furnace of the kiln and, afterwards, sacrifice the usual sheep and pig in front of the furnace door. Then he told the girl to go to bed early and to rise early the next morning in order to bring food to the workmen and to summon them to the sacrifice.

The two girls went to bed, but it was Tshai's daughter, over-excited at the thought of the sacrificial feast, who could not sleep. And it was she who slipped out early the next morning to bring the workmen their breakfast and summon them to the sacrifice. The workmen, forewarned by Tshai, were awaiting the girl, so as soon as his daughter arrived they cast her alive into the furnace. In the meantime Tshai had gone to the girls' room to waken the one he had purchased and to send her on her way to her death before anyone else stirred. He was appalled to find no sign of his daughter and hastened to the kiln in time to be met by the workmen on their way to report that his orders had been carried out. The wretched man, overcome by grief, broke down and wept.

Popular myths of the great gods

There are, naturally, many popular tales about deities, not all of them particularly respectful. Some certainly derive from Buddhist canonical sources, or later tales devised as glosses upon the canon. Others seem to be simple expressions of the peasant's eternal hope for better things in a future existence. A typical version of such a story is to be found in a tale from central China quoted by Eberhard, which explains how the kitchen-god came to be appointed.

THE KITCHEN-GOD

The kitchen-god was once no more than a poor mason who seemed fated to be unsuccessful all his life. At last his circumstances became so desperate that he was forced to sell his wife into marriage with another man. Now it so happened that one day he went to work for the man who had become his wife's new husband, but he no longer recognised her. His wife, however, still had him much in mind and, although she could not help him overtly, she resolved to do so by stealth. She baked some sesame cakes and into each one she placed a piece of money, for her new family was quite well-to-do. When he came to leave, having finished the work for which he had been called, she gave him the cakes for his journey home, but did not mention their secret ingredient. On the way the mason stopped at a wayside teahouse to break his journey. Here another traveller asked him for one of the cakes, a request which the mason gladly agreed to. The other bit into the cake and found the money, but said nothing to the mason about it. Instead, he persuaded him to part with the rest of the cakes for a modest sum. The mason, in accordance with his characteristic ill-fortune, thus parted with the gift that his ex-wife had given him out of love, while thinking that he had done well to have obtained a modest amount for the cakes. Later, when he learnt what his wife had done, he recognised that there was no point in his continued existence. He therefore killed himself. But the ruler of Heaven, acknowledging his honesty and goodness, appointed him as the kitchen-deity.

THE TWO GODS OF THE SOIL

Another tale shows deities in a somewhat odd light. It appears that there were once two gods of the soil, one on the northern mountain in a certain district, and one on the southern. But their shrines were remote, the district poor and sparsely inhabited. As a result offerings were very few and far between; in fact, both the deities were near to starvation. One day a boy passed by the shrine of the southern deity, who stretched out his hand and touched the boy's body so that when the lad returned home his body began to burn all over and he fell into a high fever. As his family worried over the boy, they heard a voice from the boy's body say that the illness was caused by mountain spirits, that the speaker was the deity of the southern mountain who would cure the ill, and that they should go to his temple, cut off a piece from

the camphor tree in front of the shrine and give an infusion made from the wood to the sick boy. The family did as they were instructed and the boy swiftly recovered. To show their gratitude the family sent food and other kinds of offering to the deity who, delighted by the success of his strategy, sent his servant to invite his fellow from the northern mountain to have dinner.

His guest was most impressed by the repast and enquired how it had come about. The southern mountain spirit explained in a suitably off-hand manner how he had achieved his success and the deity of the northern mountain resolved to adopt a similar strategy. As luck would have it, his chance occurred the very next day and he was able to touch a passing cowherd. The lad returned home, fell ill and, at once, the deity of the northern mountain entered his body to issue instructions to the stricken family, ordering them to give the sick boy an infusion of camphor wood. The father quickly hurried to the shrine to carry out the deity's orders, but, alas, there was no camphor tree by the northern shrine. He saw the image itself was of camphor wood, but was naturally reluctant to inflict a visible mutilation upon the image so, lifting its gown, he sliced some wood from the buttocks of the deity. The sick boy was brought back to health, but as the family was unbelievably poor and had nothing for themselves it never occurred to them that it was fitting to offer foodstuffs to the deity. There was no offering at all: the god remained hungry and not unnaturally wrathful, not least because of the success which his opposite number had achieved with the same gambit. Finally he made his way painfully across to the abode of the deity of the southern mountain, where he was received in some surprise. After he had explained his sad circumstances the god of the southern mountain laughed unceasingly and between guffaws said: 'Brother, fancy not remembering that there was no camphor tree by your temple. If one is hurt through one's own stupidity, there is no point in blaming others.'

A phoenix or *feng huang*, emblem of the south, of the *yin* principle and of the Empress, which in popular mythology was believed to mark the place where treasure was buried. One of a pair of phoenixes in thin gold sheet. Thang dynasty. Seattle Art Museum.

Goddess holding in her hand the Ju-i, the Precious Stone of the Pearly Emperor Yu-huang. The crayfish on which she stands is, like all fish, an emblem of wealth, regeneration, harmony and connubial bliss. British Museum.

The spring fishing festival of south China villages, derived from the seasonal marriage festivals of prehistoric times and akin to the annual offerings made by fishing communities to Ho Po, Count of the River. The dragon represents the ruler of the watery deep. Dish, famille verte. Reign of Chhien Lung. Victoria and Albert Museum.

The Assembly of the Immortals by the Lake of Gems, or Green Jade Lake in the palace grounds of Hsi Wang Mu. While some approach, others are already seated on an island feasting on the peaches of immortality. The cranes are symbolic of long life. Anonymous painting. Late Ming. British Museum.

The heavenly empire

So far we have been concerned with cosmology and cosmography, with the little that has survived of Chinese ideas about human origins and the creation of living things. But side by side with this mythology there is another system of more direct concern to men in their everyday affairs. If it be true that men create gods in their own image, then the Chinese made a most tidy business of their theogony since the divine world is but a recreation of the earthly bureaucracy on a heavenly scale.

The Supreme Emperor

Imperial China was ruled by the emperor under the protection of Heaven and by the agency of a complex and all-embracing bureaucracy, while Heaven itself was under a supreme sovereign the August Personage of Jade Yu-ti. In some traditions Yu-ti was also the creator of men, having modelled them in clay; but while they were drying in the sun some got wet: these are the halt and the sick. Yu-ti dwelt in a palace, just like his earthly counterpart, with a door-keeper and court functionaries, and had ministers who presided over the various departments concerned with human activities. His wife was Wang Mu niang-niang, another form of Hsi Wang Mu who presided over the West and lived by Mount Khun-lun. It was to this Supreme Emperor that the earthly ruler made the twice yearly sacrifices at the Altar of Heaven in Peking. These sacrifices ended with the setting up of the Republic in 1912, although they were to persist in Annam, where the court rituals were almost wholly Chinese in manner until the Second World War. The Supreme Emperor was, however, concerned only with the emperor's affairs: it was his ministers who dealt with the problems of lesser mortals. There were also members of the hierarchy charged with the affairs of such natural phenomena as sun, moon, stars and winds, a system which in many instances diverged quite considerably from that which we have already considered.

Household and personal gods

The Supreme Emperor had a doorkeeper for his palace, an armed functionary who served as sentinel and porter. But the dwelling of every Chinese was similarly protected: indeed each household had a divine as well as a human set of inhabitants. Each of the leaves of the double entrance door was protected by a separate guardian, while each lesser entrance, to the sides and rear, had a spirit guard for its single leaf. The Lord and Lady of the Bed presided over the bedchamber while the kitchen was the domain of the kitchen-god. The kitchen-god's role was considerably more extensive than his title might suggest, for it was he who every New Year's Eve went to Heaven to report to the Supreme Being on the behaviour of each member of the household. Hence honey and sticky confections were deemed suitable offerings for him – that his lips might be sealed and his revelations thus impeded. There was even a goddess to preside over the latrines. Inevitably one is reminded of the host of deities which oversaw every aspect of life in pagan Rome from conception to death. And, just as in Rome so in China there were gods especially charged with the oversight of a man's career, and with the different aspects of a woman's life.

We have no complete list of the ancient gods of China, if ever such a thing existed. Indeed, it is doubtful whether anyone has compiled a complete roll of those who still existed in this century for there were countless local differences and minor variations. Their origin can be traced to an amalgam of Buddhist and Taoist sources, with elements from much older traditions which contributed to what was in effect a new religion of the people.

In addition to the deities who safeguarded the parts of the house, there

Far left. Fairy with a basket. Though many fairies were benefactors of mankind, men had to treat them warily, for spirits of evil intent masquerading as beautiful women seduced men and so redeemend themselves at their victims' expense. Ivory. National Gallery, Prague.

The kitchen-god and his consort. He was the most important of the domestic deities, who received offerings twice a month and a special feast of honey at the New Year in order to seal his lips before he went to render his yearly report to Heaven. Paper image designed to be fixed over the kitchen stove. Horniman Museum.

Door-ring holder in the shape of a monstrous tiger head. The tiger was able to repel demons over which the domestic gods had no power, and his protection was particularly required on the fifth day of the fifth month. Six Dynasties period, A.D. 221-581. Cleveland Museum of Art.

Wine pot in the form of the character *fu*, Happiness. Though an abstract force, *fu* was thought to be within the gift of the individual's personal deities. Happiness itself was also personified in the god Fu-hsing, who was a deified magistrate called Yang Chheng, who saved the people of Hunan from the emperor Wu-ti's intolerable levy in the sixth century A.D. Victoria and Albert Museum.

was a local deity whose care was the house's situation. Then there was the god of wealth and the three gods of happiness: to all these ritual cults were offered at fixed seasons. In the family shrine the ancestral tablets brought to the living generations the spiritual presence of the ancestors, who served as a link with the other world. Each of the deities had an image in front of which incense could be offered. Those of the door-gods and Tsao Chun, the god of the kitchen, were of paper, fixed to the door-leaves and above the kitchen stove. For the other gods there were figurines, though in orthodox Confucian families these were frowned upon, a fact which does not seem to have prevented women in such households from having an image of the Buddhist, and therefore heterodox, goddess Kuan Yin. In strict Buddhist or Taoist households on the other hand, where figurines and statues were acceptable, the god of literature, Wen-chhang ta-ti, had only a tablet inscribed with his title.

Although the pantheon showed such variations, following regional or social distinctions, the whole hierarchy is best seen as a well organised divine bureaucracy with well established grades. These were drawn from Buddhist and Taoist systems as well as from the secular imperial order. Thus we find Buddhas and Bodhisattvas, Arhats, Venerable Celestial Beings, Immortals, Emperors, Empresses, Kings, Gods and Goddesses. Within the system there was a more or less fixed establishment but the individual divinities who filled the specific posts might change, either as their popularity increased or diminished or because of regional variations in cult practices.

Many of the deities were historical or semi-historical figures who became divine because of their terrestrial achievements. These sometimes received promotion within the hierarchy by official terrestrial decree as in the case of Kuan Ti which we shall discuss below.

Kuan Ti, The God of War

Kuan Ti, in whose honour more than 1,600 official temples, to say nothing of countless minor shrines in Manchu-

A judge of Hell. Hell, like Heaven, was ruled by an elaborate bureaucracy where the punishments meted out to the evil were exactly calculated to match their crimes. Pottery statue. Late Ming.

Kuan Yin seated on Pu-to Shan, the famous Buddhist sanctuary in the Chusan islands to which the goddess was borne on a water lily. Despite her expression of abstraction, Kuan Yin was known and loved beyond the other deities, for she postponed her own eternal bliss in order to help mankind and had mercy on all who called upon her. *c.* eighteenth-nineteenth centuries. A.D. Buddhist scroll painting.

times were dedicated, was originally a kind of Robin Hood figure. He was one of three heroes whose adventures are recounted in the *Romance of the Three Kingdoms*, a pseudo-historical account of events at the end of the Later Han dynasty, written at the beginning of the Ming period. Kuan Chung was a native of Shansi who was forced to flee through the pass to Shensi after killing an official for an act of sexual tyranny. There he fell in with a butcher, Chang Fei, and a peddlar of straw sandals, Liu Pei, who was to be the founder of the Shu Han dynasty of Szechwan. In a peach-orchard belonging to Chang Fei, the three took an oath of loyalty to one another and of service to the state. The story tells of their adventuring and crusading together and of the virtues of Kuan Chung until in the end he was captured and executed by one of his opponents, Sun Chhuan, in A.D. 219. The virtues of Kuan Chung were later recognised and he was awarded the rank of Duke posthumously by an imperial decree in A.D. 1120, a rank which was upgraded to that of Prince in A.D. 1128.

Some years later the Yuan emperor Wen promoted him again to the rank of Warrior Prince and Bringer of Civilisation, which title he held until A.D. 1594 when the Ming emperor Wan Li conferred upon the dead hero the title Faithful and Loyal Great Deity (*ti*), Supporter of Heaven, Protector of the Realm. During Manchu times his cult reached its peak and it is believed that he appeared in the sky in the support of the imperial forces in A.D. 1856. He was adopted as patron of many trades and professions, while the sword of the public executioner was kept in his temple enclosure. Here, after an execution, the supervising magistrate would make offerings so that the spirit of the executed man might not pursue him to his home.

But hero-gods such as Kuan Ti could also be explained in religious bureaucratic terms. For just as secular bureaucrats were sent into exile from the court, so immortal administrators guilty of some celestial offence might be sent from the heavenly court to spend a per-

iod of exile on earth. Then their military or civil achievements, which were to earn them deification, could be explained as the deeds by which they atoned for their misdemeanours and regained admission to the divine civil service. Only the highest grades, Buddhas, Bodhisattvas and Venerable Celestial Beings, appear to have been exempt from such hazards of advancement and demotion. In their case alone the Buddhist concept of Enlightenment operated (even for the Taoist *thien-tsun*) and they had reached the point of no return. But they too were conceived of in personal terms, as were all the deities of the popular pantheon.

The major deities, it was felt, could not be present at all the many images in their many temples. Such deities were allowed to appoint deputies, the souls of the just, who could act on their behalf, and give account of the ceremonies and rites in the temples to which they were appointed. As compensation they were entitled to receive a proportion of the offerings. Though Chinese popular religion was always concerned above all with personal deities, this is certainly not to say that impersonal forces played no part in Chinese life. Such obscure, powerful and ill-defined forces as Happiness *fu* and Destiny *ming* affected each individual, but these were generally thought of as being within the gift of the individual's personal deities, who might vary each person's share in them as they pleased. Only *feng-shui*, Wind and Water, those mysterious natural forces which influenced sites and what was connected with them, whose powers it was the function of the geomancer to determine, seem to have been conceived of as wholly impersonal and outside the sphere of the gods.

The sky-god and his bureaucrat

Who then were these personal deities and what were their functions? Originally, there had been a supreme deity Shang Ti who was a sky-god. His function had been to preside over a hierarchy, but his divine nature tended to be eroded by Confucian rationalism and he had become known simply as Thien

Sky. Even in this role, however, he retained his importance, for Sky sees and hears everything: men may whisper but to Sky the sound is as loud as thunder; nothing escapes his eye. Despite the efforts of atheistic scholars, therefore, Sky remained a deity and as such was the supreme figure in the popular pantheon ultimately responsible for individual destiny: each blade of grass has its share of the dew. To him was also attributed the title of the Taoist supreme being, the August of Jade Yu-huang, a title of ancient origins, which received imperial recognition after the deity had appeared twice to Sung emperors. There was nothing capricious about Yu-huang's rule: the seasons followed their established plan; *yin* and *yang* were in balance; the good rewarded, the evil punished. But like other supreme deities, Yu-huang became remote and it became more usual to offer ritual to his door-keeper (a reflection no doubt of the necessary preliminaries to obtaining a boon or even justice from a terrestrial functionary). This official, the Transcendent Dignitary, drove off evil spirits from the celestial palace and became a popular figure in the pantheon. Nor did Yu-huang occupy himself any longer with natural phenomena: the charge of these was assigned to different gods: the Count of the Wind, the Master of the Rain, the Lord of the Lightning (the celestial executioner who alone among these figures persisted as a living god in popular belief).

Yu-huang's principal aide was Tung-yo ta-ti, the Great Emperor of the Eastern Peak, the birthplace of *yang*. As Yu-huang's deputy he was seen as head of a ministry with no fewer than seventy-five departments which were occupied with the supervision of every aspect of life on earth. Here were fixed the times of birth and death, the course of life for all living creatures, as well as an inspectorate responsible for the oversight of terrestrial deities. Two points are of note. First that human and animal life were equally the concern of Tung-yo ta-ti's bureaucrats, recruited from amongst the souls of the virtuous dead. Human and animal life formed a con-

tinuum because of the Buddhist belief in reincarnation, adopted in its entirety by the Taoists and firmly installed in the popular religion. In this system rebirth as an animal was a typical punishment for an erring human: reincarnation in human form a suitable reward for animal virtue. Another reward or punishment was an increase or reduction of the normal life span: such variations were made at the time of birth by one of the departments in the ministry. The second point is that since all life was the concern of this ministry there were departments specially concerned with such categories as thieves and murderers. So powerful a deity inevitably attracted great popular attention and in Peking, where his temple at one time had eighty departments, his role as a giver of offspring was recognised by women who sought a son. The ritual was to offer incense and then to take home one of the small dolls deposited as a thank-offering by those whose desire had already been granted. When the son wished for was born the mother returned the original doll to the temple with a second as her own token of gratitude.

The gods of the soil: district administrators

As we have already seen, the high role attributed to the sky-deity in ancient China was paralleled by a cult of the god of the soil. We should expect that as the cult of the sky-deity continued, though the main cult was now centred about his principal deputy, so would that of the earth-god, though it too perhaps in modified form. And this indeed was the case. The place of the great god of the soil had been taken by a whole series of gods of the wall and moat. This was Chheng-huang, responsible in each district for the land and its inhabitants, who received from local officials the petitions which in earlier, feudal, times had been addressed by rulers to the god of the soil. Chheng-huang was thought to control the ravages of wild beasts or beasts that might destroy the harvest, to break droughts or halt excessive rain and to bring peace and prosperity to the people in his dis-

Figure of Shou-lao, god of long life and originally a stellar deity, who headed one of the seventy-five departments under the jurisdiction of the Great Emperor of the Eastern Peak. It was he who fixed the times of a man's death, inscribing it in his tablets at the moment of birth. Occasionally he was known to change his mind on the entreaty of the parents. He is usually shown smiling. The panels on his robe resemble those of costly silk tapestry and symbolic patterns worn by the courtiers at the imperial court on earth. Reign of Khang Hsi. Victoria and Albert Museum.

Li Thieh-kuai, a pupil of Lao Tzu, who lost his mortal body while his soul was visiting the Master. His soul was reborn into the body of a beggar with an iron crutch. He became one of the Eight Taoist Immortals. Taoist scroll painting.

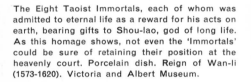

The Eight Taoist Immortals, each of whom was admitted to eternal life as a reward for his acts on earth, bearing gifts to Shou-lao, god of long life. As this homage shows, not even the 'Immortals' could be sure of retaining their position at the heavenly court. Porcelain dish. Reign of Wan-li (1573-1620). Victoria and Albert Museum.

trict. At the same time he had some concern with the disposal of the souls of the dead, once Yen-lo had summoned the soul to appear before him. Chheng-huang had the right to make sure that Yen-lo's emissaries had acted properly in carrying off that particular one of the inhabitants under his protection. The two servants of the king of the under-world had therefore to present the soul in question at the court of Chheng-huang, who would satisfy himself of the correctness of the summons: that the calculations of the department in Tung-yo ta-ti's ministry concerned with the length of the creature's days had been properly complied with. He then carried out a preliminary judgment, committing the soul to the final jurisdiction of Yen-lo, the Buddhist Yama, king of the dead.

As we might expect, the district god of wall and moat had his own servants, of whom the best known were Po lao-ye and Hei lao-ye, Mr White and Mr Black, whose garments matched their titles and whose role was to watch all activities in their town or district by day and by night respectively. And, following a pattern with which we are becoming familiar, each Chheng-huang had a number of subordinate deities, *Thu-ti chen* (*chen* being the title of the lowest grade of divinity), of whom Maspero wrote:

Each country village, each quarter and each street of a town, each temple, each public building, each bridge, each field has its own; they have their temple, their chapel, their shrine or at least an inscribed tablet according to their importance. In the villages their role is the same as that of Chheng-huang in the towns; they maintain the register of inhabitants and that is why whenever there is a death a group of women from the family concerned goes to announce it to the deity in his temple on the night following the death, weeping and burning gold and silver paper. Chheng-huang and the subordinate godlings had no doubt been chthonic deities like the original god of the soil; but during the long period after the cult's appearance and development in the first few centuries of the Christian era they became increasingly anthropomorphised and were generally thought of as district administrators who, after death, had simply been transferred from the terrestrial to the heavenly oversight of the same district, a divine prefect. As a nineteenth-century Chinese viceroy explained, the Chheng-huang actually presided over the administration of a district: he gave happiness to the good and unhappiness to the wicked. He had a special responsibility for those without descendants, who therefore lacked people to make offerings to them. On the occasion of the Seventh Month festival, while the god was taken in procession round his town, the populace made offerings which were treated as being intended for this unfortunate category of spirits.

The Chheng-huang of each place had the rank appropriate to the size and dignity of his charge and was treated as its spiritual magistrate. He was thus frequently consulted by the magistracy in instances where there was difficulty in establishing the truth in a case. He might also be approached by lay people, as happened with the Chheng-huang of Yen Chheng city. An orphan, brought up by his uncle and aunt, was accused of stealing a golden hairpin from the latter. To prove his innocence the youth went to swear an oath before the image of Chheng-huang. As he left the temple he stumbled and fell, precisely the fate he had invoked should he have been guilty of the theft. He was therefore driven out by his relations. By virtue and industry, however, he achieved success and became a mandarin. Returning to his old home, he went back to the temple and slept there, the standard method of consulting the god, in order to seek out the truth of the matter. In a dream he learnt that the pin was, in fact, under the floorboards in his relatives' house. It was duly discovered, and the young mandarin went back to the temple to offer thanks and reproaches to Chheng-huang for finally revealing the truth. 'You caused me to fall,' he said, 'so that people believed

An Arhat dreaming. By the exercise of virtue and the practice of contemplation Arhats, the immediate disciples of Buddha, could attain the reward of a beatific state, which increasingly resembled that of the Taoist Immortals, who lived on dew or on pure jade and floated on the mountain air. Similarly any mortal could by virtue obtain divine aid and better his worldly position. Eighteenth century. Buddhist scroll painting.

A *lung*, or dragon, which in China was regarded as a beneficent spirit of the moist, *yang* principle, dwelling either in the clouds or in the waters. There were five sorts: heavenly, which guarded the mansions of the gods; spiritual, which controlled winds and rains, and would only accidentally cause flooding; earthly, which cleared rivers and deepened seas; those of hidden treasure; and imperial dragons marked, as here, by their five claws, the others having four. Porcelain dish. Reign of Khang Hsi. Metropolitan Museum of Art.

Kuan Ti with Chang Fei on his left and Liu Pei on his right. Known as the Three Brothers of the Peach-orchard after the place where they swore friendship, they were renowned for their exploits in upholding justice. Chang Fei, a butcher, was eight feet tall, with a panther's head, a tiger's beard and round eyes. His voice was like thunder. Eighteenth century. Taoist scroll painting.

in my guilt. Now you accept my offerings. Are you not ashamed? You have no face!' At these words the plaster from the face of the image fell to the floor and despite attempts to repair it, the statue remained faceless from then on. Of course, people tried to excuse the deity, saying that he had been away from the temple on the day that the orphan first approached him, and that the minor spirits had caused the boy to stumble out of malice. But it was curious that it was not possible to restore his face.

Guardians of the home

Tung-yo ta-ti and Chheng-huang were concerned with human and animal destiny and how the destined existence was carried out. But the detailed control and manipulation of this was in the hands of a multiplicity of other deities. As we have already noted the house itself was the province of a number of separate specialists of whom the most important, without any doubt, was the kitchen-god. He seems to have been originally a Taoist deity and has been described as the Chief of the Secret Police to the Taoist supreme being. Offerings were made to his paper representation twice a month, at the new and the full moon, and he was the object of special attentions just before the New Year when he went to Heaven to render his report of the family whose most intimate observer he was.

According to legend his cult developed in Han times. A certain Taoist priest called Li Shao-chun obtained from him the double boon of perpetual youth and freedom from the need for food. The priest then went to the emperor Hsiao Wu-ti (140-86 B.C.) and promised him all kinds of benefit, including those alchemical secrets which it was believed the mythical emperor Huang Ti had possessed, if the cult of the kitchen-god under the direction of Li Shao-chun were to receive imperial patronage and support. After the priest had succeeded in contriving an appearance of the god before the emperor, the latter made a sacrifice to him, fully persuaded that he too would receive the pill which granted

immortality and the secret of making gold. When the expected rewards failed to materialise, the emperor grew sceptical and the frantic priest sought to contrive another miracle like that of the god's manifestation. He therefore caused an ox to swallow a piece of silk on which he had written a few phrases. He then predicted that if the ox were to be slain, magical writings would be found in its stomach. Everything turned out as the priest had predicted, but unfortunately the emperor recognised the writing as that of Li Shao-chun and ordered his execution. Since the god was already installed in favour, however, his cult continued to flourish despite his patron's ignominious end.

The kitchen-god was not one of the Five Gods, the Wu-sseu of ancient China, to whom sacrifices were made. It is likely, however, that his cult was already established in ancient times though not yet in its developed and popular style. The earliest domestic gods were the god of the interior courtyard who served as the god of the soil for the house, the smallest territorial unit; the god of the entrance door, of the back door, of the aisles (the traditional house had a number of aisles under a single roof); and the god of the well. In post-Han times the importance of these various deities changed considerably and the kitchen-god, indisputably the most important of them, was thought of as their chief and leader. Next in standing were the Men Shen, two deities to be seen, one each, on the leaves of the front door, where their vividly coloured images were attached. In popular belief one of them was good, the other evil, although in their later forms they were officially supposed to be two translated generals, Yu Che and Chhin Shu-pao, who heroically defended the gates of the imperial palace against demonic assault in Thang China. Fully accoutred and armed with halberds they barred the entrance to the house against all evil spirits and against demons bringing pestilence. The back door was guarded by yet another deity.

The story goes that the emperor Tai Tsung (A.D. 627-50) lay sick in his palace and thought that he heard demons prowling in his bedroom. He had tried unsuccessfully to obtain a reprieve for a dragon which had distributed rain erroneously, a fault for which he had been sentenced to decapitation by the August Personage of Jade. The dragon was haunting him in reproach. When he informed the empress and the doctors who were called to treat him of this, saying that even when the days were peaceful, the nights were full of demonic assaults, they were much concerned and the two heroes volunteered to defend the door of the imperial bedchamber at night. Their watch was successful and the night passed without disturbance. They continued their vigil for subsequent nights until the emperor, anxious for their well-being, ordered them to desist, but, for safety's sake, to paint their portraits, in full panoply, upon the leaves of the door. These substitute sentinels were effective for a number of nights, but then similar demonic assaults began through the back entrance to the palace. Thereupon the minister Wei Cheng offered to guard the rear gate in the same manner as Chhin Shu-pao and Yu Che had guarded the front. The effort was successful and henceforward Tai Tsung's nights were undisturbed. As a result the brightly painted figures of the Men Shen, renewed each New Year, at a time when all the household deities received special attention, were to be seen on every door.

This heroic pair were not, however, the original guardians of the entrance. They were replacements for an earlier couple, Shen Shu and Yu Lei. Once, many millennia ago, an immense peach tree grew on Mount Tu Shuo in the Eastern Sea. Its branches covered many acres, and the lowest of these, which inclined towards the north-east, served as a doorway for devils *kuei*. Two spirits were stationed by the branch bridge to seize those demons which had harmed men and hand them over to were-tigers for destruction. Huang Ti had pictures of the two spirits painted on peach-wood and hung above doors to keep off demons. Gradually the custom grew

of depicting Shen Shu and Yu Lei, armed with bow and arrows and spears, the one on the left, the other on the right of doors. These figures, like those of later times, were painted on paper and stuck on the leaves of the doors.

Demon spirits

These *kuei* (spirits) were one category among a number of beings harmful to mankind. The souls of those who met death by drowning or who committed suicide, and were thus unable to attain a further incarnation, were

Deity of fearsome aspect whose task was to repel demons attempting to approach the house. Several lines of defence against demons were placed round each house. Stoneware roof tile of the Ming dynasty

Sword made of coins threaded with string an
hung on the curtains of a cot to protect newbor
babies from the *thou-tzu kuei*, the spirits of wome
who had died without children and who tried t
steal infants. Wellcome Medical Museum.

A pair of cranes which may have served as an incense burner. Cranes were symbolic of happiness and also of literary elegance, so that they were appropriate images both of Fu-hsing and of Wenchhang, god of literature. National Gallery, Prague.

forced to return as dangerous ghosts t earth. The drowned were freed fror their wanderings and returned to th normal reincarnation cycle when th death of another mortal at the site o their own drowning liberated them Suicides seem never to have been abl to escape from the special town t which all suicides were consigned. I was generally believed that these ghost were bound to wander because thei sudden and violent deaths meant tha they had not completed the life-cycl assigned to them by the bureaucrat of Tung-yo ta-ti. In consequence the had to live out the balance of thei given days as ghosts until they wer permitted to enter limbo and be reborn

The *kuei* were not alone, however There were many other maleficen creatures, some of which were animal who, as they grew old, developed th power to transform themselves int human forms. Of these the best know were the foxes who became beautifu young men and women, seduced thos of the opposite sex and then slowl consumed their being in order to prolon their own lives. Such beasts wer believed to survive for eight hundred or a thousand years at the expense of succession of victims.

The emperor Yu was said, as we hav seen, to have observed a white fox as a auspicious omen when seeking for bride, but in general the beast wa considered inauspicious and evil. Thi was in part because it lies up by da and moves at night, thereby receivin an excess of the dark, inferior femal half of the *yin-yang* entity. On the othe hand it is this avoidance of the ligh which, according to some sources, wa responsible for the asserted longevit of the fox, a characteristic which in thi

An ancestress depicted, according to custom, in her marriage robes. The ancestors were the link through which the family approached the gods. The portraits were carefully preserved but brought out only on the first six days of the New Year. More importance was attached to male ancestors, but an ancestress could intercede on behalf of women desiring children. Taoist scroll painting.

view it shares with other nocturnal creatures such as badgers (also ill-omened and often confused with the fox in legends) and moles. The flesh of the fox was most important in the Chinese traditional pharmacopaeia despite (or perhaps because of) the creature's ill-repute. Its entrails too had their medicinal values, while the saliva of the fox 'gathered in a decoy-jar with a narrow neck and having a bait inside, is given as a love-potion to cold wives'. Further the fox was thought to have a mysterious power to make fire, either by banging its brush upon the ground or by emitting a fire-ball from its mouth. As a creature often found inhabiting crevices in ancient tombs, it was easy enough for the fox to become associated with the spirits of the dead, whose wrongs it was thought to avenge against the living who had been responsible for them. But the fox itself, possessor of a power to foresee the future and thus its own death, was also the epitome of a seemly death. 'The fox died correctly with his head on the mound' is a phrase used to describe such a proper death and refers to an ancient belief.

There were other demon animals and even objects which had to viewed with extreme circumspection. The danger was always when the object in question was old, and more especially if it had had human associations over a long period of time. The statues of horses before the ancient tombs of high officials were able to journey at night and even to take human form. The mounds which supported funerary steles, like ancient porcelain head-rests, were possessed of sinister powers, as were ancient trees or particular stones. Some of these too were able to transform themselves into human form and prey upon mankind.

Jade carving of a Lohan, one who is about to attain Enlightenment. The use of jade for such subjects and the title August of Jade or Jade Emperor for the supreme deity was natural to the Chinese, who considered this rare, beautiful and indestructible material to have magical and curative properties. It was the food of the Taoist Immortals. Reign of Chhien Lung (1736-95). Metropolitan Museum of Art, New York.

Huang Ti, the Yellow Emperor, discussing with Shen-nung his classic book on medicine, supposed to contain the secret of immortality which he had learned from Thai-i. The pill of immortality also conferred the ability to make gold, and to obtain it was the aim of many emperors throughout Chinese history. Figures carved in ivory. Wellcome Medical Museum.

The souls of men eaten by tigers became bond slaves to the beasts that swallowed them and hunted other men on their behalf. They hoped thereby to gain their own release, for having died violently they were *kuei* and removed from the cycle of reincarnation until they could find another soul to take their place.

Fearsome though these demons might be, the Men Shen were usually capable of repelling them. The kitchen-god and others of the household deities could dispose of most of those who passed the guardians of the doors, especially if they were supported by amulets and charms strategically disposed about the house – some of general protective intention, some specific for certain evil spirits. Further defences were available in the strategic situation of the house at the end of a street or beside a bridge, since spirits were reluctant to cross flowing water. A brick screen before the entrance, or a simple single stone would serve to deter many of the demons, who were apparently bound to travel in straight lines. A net suspended about the cradle or the smoke from burning slippers would protect the infant during its first hundred days from the attack of *thou-tzu kuei*, young women who died before marriage and were therefore eager to steal babies in place of those of whom they had been deprived.

Astrologers and other specialists of the horoscope were able, by their calculations, to warn of especially dangerous days and periods in the life of the young when precautions against demonic attack were particularly necessary. Should such precautions fail, then Taoist exorcists would perform their rituals to expel the maleficent spirits and exorcise the victim. For those who voyaged outside the protection of the domestic deities, there were calendars which listed the days of great risk, the worst being the fifth of the fifth month, when drawings of tigers (in their apotropaic or deterrent role) were fixed to doors and walls, and the character tiger written upon the foreheads of young children. On such perilous days, the prudent man stayed at home and avoided new enterprises.

Men and animals

Lao Tzu, the first teacher of Taoism, who resided in the Taoist Third Heaven. In his popular form as Lao Chun he was a powerful sorcerer. His intervention led to the capture of Monkey, but not even his furnace could prevail against Monkey's double protection of immortality. Taoist scroll painting

There are many other stories which deal with relations between humans and animals. These serve various ends. One, for instance, explains why monkeys have red-ringed eyes and naked buttocks. These characteristics are the result of devices used by a human bride to elude her monkey husband, aided by her mother. The husband, like the forsaken merman, is left weeping and crying: 'Monkey wife, monkey wife, it is unnatural to abandon your children. They are in tears and your husband mourns.'

How the oxen twisted their horns

There are many myths about oxen. One rather charming one from Yunnan sets out to explain why it is that some cattle have twisted horns.

There was once a Thai girl who, being thirsty, drank from a mountain stream. And as she drank she noticed a vegetable root drifting in the water whose leaves had been nibbled by some animal, but whose flesh remained whole and unharmed. She therefore peeled it and ate the inside, which was both sweet and thirst–quenching. Afterwards she became pregnant and gave birth to a baby girl. The people were pleased, for the child was sweet-voiced and a beautiful dancer. All the men, both young and old, fell victims to her beauty; but when the young men learnt that she had no father they could no longer risk being seen in her company, while the women cursed her as being begotten out of marriage.

The child grew unhappy and asked her mother why she did not have a father as other children did. Finally, her mother told her the story of her conception, adding that she was certain that even if her daughter were to see her father, she would be sure to dislike him, for he was bound to be very ugly. But the child insisted that, even if ugly, the man would still be her father. So then the mother revealed that the child's father was in fact a holy ox, who had told her in a dream on the day of the child's birth that it was he who had eaten the leaves of the vegetable, and that he dwelt in the midst of the mountains. The child asked why her mother had made no attempt to find the ox, and the mother explained that she did not feel able to leave her child among the hostile villagers while she went on such a search. So the child resolved to go herself in search of her father and asked her mother how she would recognise him. 'Take roots with you, my child, and feed them to the oxen that you meet upon your way in the mountains. When you find an ox that eats only the leaves, that will be your father.'

The next morning the child set off into the mountains and searched until she found, deep in the mountains, an ox which ate only the leaves of the proferred root. She followed him till she came to a cave where he lived with many other magic oxen. Near the cave she found a hollow tree in which she set up house. In the mornings she cleaned out the cave where the cattle dwelt, and when they returned in the evening they were astonished to find the cave cleared of dung. This continued until one day the ox who was her father stayed behind and discovered that it was the girl who was cleaning their dwelling cave. Then he recognised his daughter.

The girl continued to live in the hollow tree until the autumn, when it began to grow cold. But despite her father's entreaties she would not return to her village, preferring to die of cold in the

The reception of the Immortals at the court of Hsi Wang Mu in preparation for the Peach Festival, which was held on the goddess's birthday every three thousand years. When Monkey stole the entire feast the Jade Emperor decided that he was beyond redemption and must be condemned to death. Scroll painting. British Museum.

Mi-lo Fo, otherwise known as Maitreya or the 'laughing Buddha', under whose presidency a heavenly committee welcomed Monkey and Thang Seng back from their successful pilgrimage. Images of the pot-bellied Mi-lo Fo, who was identified with the god of wealth, were common at the entrance to temples. Porcelain. Victoria and Albert Museum.

Lung dragon surmounted by a medallion showing the white hare of the moon standing at the foot of the Cassia tree and pounding the elixir of immortality which Heng-o is to drink, and which will turn her into an immortal toad. Detail from an eighteenth-century embroidered emperor's robe. Victoria and Albert Museum.

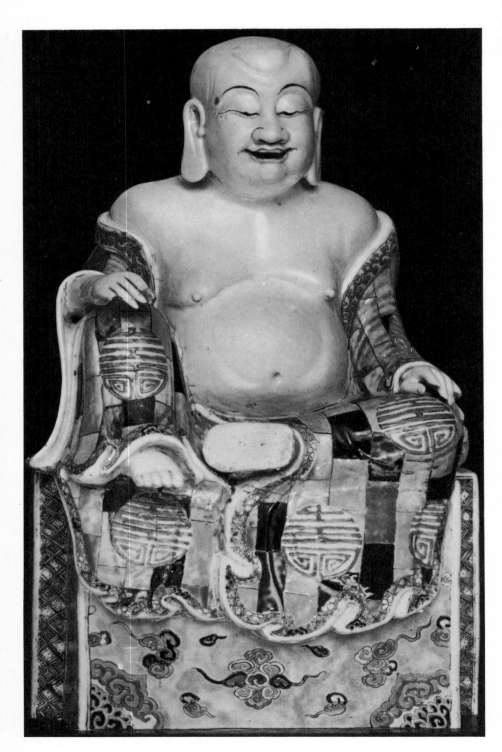

mountains to returning to the hostile villagers. Her father therefore determined to build her a home. The only building material he had was horn, so all the cattle took off their horns and gave them to the girl's father to build her a house of horn. It was quickly done and soon, when only one more horn was required to complete the very beautiful building the father ox called out 'enough'. Then those of the magic cattle who were still twisting their horns in order to take them off stopped. And that is why the horns of some cattle are straight while those of others are twisted.

The dog who married a princess

But of marriages with animals the best known tale is probably that which tells how a dog married the daughter of the Emperor of China:

The Emperor was engaged in war against a neighbouring ruler to the west. His army was so badly defeated that his generals were reluctant to continue the struggle. In the end, to embolden them, the Emperor was forced to issue a proclamation offering his daughter in marriage to the warrior who should bring him the head of the enemy chief. The proclamation was much discussed in the Chinese camp, but though the Emperor's daughter was a worthy reward in every way no one could be found bold enough to undertake the enterprise.

A large dog belonging to one of the generals heard the talk and, slipping quietly out of the camp, made his way through the enemy lines into the tent of the chief. Here he gnawed off the head of the enemy chief and returned with it to his own camp, where he laid it at the feet of the Emperor. The enemy were seen to be in confusion and soon withdrew to the rejoicing of the victorious Chinese. At this point the dog reminded the Emperor of his promise. The latter explained the impossibility of a marriage between the dog and an imperial princess, whereupon the dog proposed that he should transform himself into a man by being placed under a bell, removed from human eyes for the space of 280 days. The emperor

agreed to the proposal and for 279 days the dog remained undisturbed inside the bell. But on the two hundred and eightieth day the emperor was unable to restrain his curiosity any longer and, lifting the rim, he peeped underneath.

The dog was wholly transformed save only for his head. The spell having been broken by the Emperor's rash action, however, his daughter was now faced with a dog-headed suitor. Since the fault was entirely the Emperor's, the marriage had to take place, though the bridegroom's head was carefully covered with a red cloth for the occasion. (Some stories say that it was the bride who was veiled in red so that she might not see her husband's ugly head.) The children were fair of limb but unfortunately had their father's head. To this day, therefore, the tribesmen known as the Jung of Fuchow wear a red head-covering to disguise their features. These people still paint a dog on a screen at the time of the old-style New Year and make offerings to it, saying that it is a representation of their ancestor wh defeated the enemy from the west.

The farmer who befriended a fo:

Though many encounters with foxe were disastrous, from time to tim we come across stories where the fo pleased with its treatment, brings wealt and success to the host who has be friended it. But then friendship has it hazards.

There was once a man with an eno mous straw stack. As straw was remov ed, a hole was left in which a fox too up its home. It used to appear to th owner of the stack in the form of an ol man, a favourite transformation of foxe One day it invited the owner to visit it i its hole, which turned out to contain long set of handsomely furnished apar ments. Here superb tea and fine wine were served. The fox was wont to spen the nights away from the straw yard an admitted that he went to take wine wit friends. The owner begged to be a lowed to accompany him and to this th fox agreed, though with reluctance

Chin Shan, the Buddhist island of gold, on which stood a famous monastery. When Thang Seng was born his mother was at the mercy of her husband's murderer; on the advice of Kuan Yin she cast the infant on the waves, and he was later washed up on Chin Shan and brought up by the monks. Buddhist scroll painting.

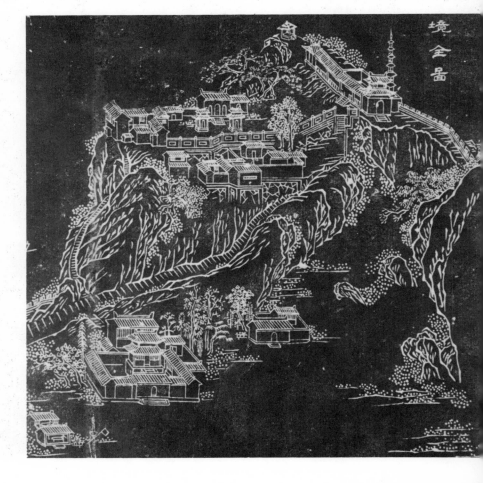

o they set off through the air until, n the time it takes to cook a pot of nillet, they reached a city where they ntered a restaurant in which a great ompany was drinking. They went nto the gallery, to which the fox rought wine and various delicacies. Then a handsomely dressed man brought dish of preserved cumquats to a table elow. The owner asked the fox to etch some, but the latter admitted that ne could not do so since he who had rought them was an upright man whom fox might not approach. His guest eflected that in frequenting the com- any of the fox he had lost the right o be considered upright and resolved hat henceforward he would follow a ath of probity. As he thus reflected e fell at once from the gallery into the ompany below and the fox disappeared. ooking up he saw that there was no allery, only a large rafter on which e must have been sitting. The aston- shed company listened to his account f his adventure and then collected noney to pay for his return home, for he

was a thousand *li* from his house and straw yard.

Monkey

Of the purely animal stories, that of Monkey is certainly the best known. The manner in which the monkey became part of the Chinese pantheon is told in the *Hsi yu chi*, an account of a journey to the Western Paradise in order to obtain the Buddhist scriptures for the Emperor of China. The story is, in fact, a version of the true story of the in- troduction of Buddhism into China. It tells of Thang Seng, a pilgrim (the historical Hsuan Tsang), who went to India, the land of the Buddha, to obtain true texts of the Buddha's teachings, and died in A.D. 664. Thang Seng was accompanied on his journey by the Monkey Fairy, Sun hou-tzu, who like human beings was prone to evil, and Chu Pa-chieh, a Pig-spirit represent- ing the coarser elements in the human spirit.

Monkey was born from an egg which had been fertilised by the wind as it

Pair of monkey vases. A number of myths centre on monkeys and their relations with human beings. They were subject to the same hardships and frailties as human beings; the Monkey Fairy Sun hou-tzu, who represented human nature and its propensity to evil, was popular for getting away with it and vindicating his nature by his services on the journey to the Western Paradise. Porcelain, famille rose. Reign of Chhien Lung.

ne of the Men Shen, door guardians, deified
enerals of the Thang dynasty. Armed with hal-
erds, arrows and magic symbols, they guarded
e house against evil spirits and pestilence.
uch paper images of the Men Shen were pasted to
e door during the New Year celebrations. Paint-
g from Soochow. Nineteenth century.

The *chhi-lin*, a fabulous creature of good omen
which was the emblem of the upright judge Kao-yao,
and which spared the innocent but struck the guilty
with its single horn. Its appearance at the imperial
court was a sign of heavenly favour. Detail from an
early nineteenth-century chair cover. Victoria and
Albert Museum.

Kuan Ti, god of war, patron of literature, and up-holder of justice. He was a popular deity throughout China, not as a wager of war, but as a preventer of strife and protector against evil. War itself was a ritualised system of justice by ordeal. Fukien province. Reign of Khang Hsi. Victoria and Albert Museum.

lay on the peak of a mountain in Ao-lai on the eastern side of the Ocean. He became unbelievably adept at magic arts and learnt further skills from a Taoist Immortal who among other things gave him the personal name of Discoverer of Secrets, taught him to change his shape at will and to fly through the air. Monkey organised all the monkeys of the world into a kingdom and slew a monster who was persecuting them. He obtained a magic weapon from the Dragon King of the Eastern Sea with which he began to make himself master of the four quarters.

Then, at a great feast given in his honour, Monkey drank too much; while he was asleep he was seized by the servants of the king of Hell, who had him chained in the infernal regions. He broke his bonds, however, and stole the register of judgments from which he deleted his own name and that of all monkeys. As a result of all the trouble which he caused he was summoned to Heaven to explain his conduct. The Lord of Heaven made him Grand Overseer of the Heavenly Stables to keep him quiet. This succeeded until Monkey learnt of the true reasons for his appointment, when started to break up Heaven itself and then withdrew to Mount Hua-kuo. The Heavenly Host organised a siege of the mountain, but was repulsed. Finally, after Monkey had proclaimed himself Governor of Heaven and Great Saint, terms were arranged and he agreed to conform to the divine laws as Superintendent in Chief of the Heavenly Peach Garden, the source of Immortality. Unfortunately he was not invited to come to the Peach Festival and so to revenge himself he not only ate all the food and wine prepared for the feast but also stole the pills of immortality from the house of Lao Chun. As Monkey had already eaten the peaches he was thus made doubly immortal. After this he retired once again to Mount Hua-kuo. But his irresponsible behaviour had by now infuriated all the gods and goddesses. After a long siege in which Monkey employed all his magic skills to avoid defeat, he was finally captured and

brought before the Jade Emperor, who condemned him to death as a base criminal in revolt against the Heavenly Throne.

The sentence could not, however, be carried out because Monkey was protected both by the peaches and by the pills. He was handed over to Lao Chun (in fact Lao Tzu in his popular magical form) to be distilled in the alchemists' furnace. The furnace was heated to white heat for forty-nine days, but at the end of this time Monkey lifted the lid and threatened to destroy Heaven. In despair the Jade Emperor sent for the Buddha, who asked Monkey why he wished to possess Heaven. Monkey's reply was that he knew with certainty that he was sufficiently powerful to rule Heaven. When the Buddha demanded proof for this claim, Monkey explained that he was immortal, invulnerable, able to change his shape in seventy-two different ways, to fly through the air and to leap a distance of 108,000 li. The Buddha doubted whether Monkey could even jump out of the Buddha's palm, but agreed that if Monkey was successful, then he was surely entitled to rule Heaven. So Monkey leaped into the air and sprang prodigiously across Heaven to the furthest confines of the earth, where he came to rest at the base of a great mountain. Here he pissed as animals do when they wish to mark out a territory as their own. Then he returned in a single bound and confronted the Buddha. (In the more respectable texts it is said that like a genteel tourist Monkey wrote his name on one of the rocks.) But the Buddha laughed at his claim to have traversed the whole universe at a single bound and showed him that the mountain where he had pissed was but the base of one of the Buddha's fingers and that he had not even escaped from the palm of the Buddha's hand. Then the Buddha created a magic mountain and shut Monkey within it.

Here he would have remained for ever had the Bodhisattva Kuan Yin not obtained his release so that he might accompany Thang Seng on his great pilgrimage to the Western Paradise to

Temple of the Lamas in Peking. Buddhism came to China from many different sources, but the forms it adopted in China allowed it to become closely linked with Taoism. The Mongol rulers particularly encouraged Lamaism because of its magical practices.

The Hall of Annual Prayers or Temple of Heaven in Peking. Its umbrella-like blue-tiled roof is itself symbolic of the circular sky, while its three layers correspond to the Three Heavens. In this temple the Son of Heaven communed with the Supreme Emperor and received his own mandate to rule China.

Bronze dragon guarding the entrance to one of the palaces inside the Purple Forbidden City, Peking. The Forbidden City was the imperial palace itself, and the pearl placed before the dragon is the symbol of imperial treasure.

Bell of the Huai style (late Chou), decorated with dragon and *thao-thieh* motifs. Such bronze bells, oval in cross section, were used not only in the performance of music at court (which Confucians thought conducive to morality), but also played an important part in the rituals of the *wu* shamans. The bells thus acquired the supernatural qualities illustrated in the myth of the dog and the princess. Minneapolis Institute of Arts.

fetch authentic versions of the Buddha's teachings. The Monkey swore faithfully to obey his new master and to protect him from perils: this he did despite many temptations upon the way and some eighty mighty perils which the pilgrims had to undergo. On their return a last hazard awaited them when a turtle, who was conveying them and the scriptures across a flooded river, finding that Thang Seng had not yet fulfilled a vow he had made to the turtle on their outward journey, swam away and left them to sink. But they swam safely ashore and were greeted with great honours by the Emperor and the people.

Their final honours came from a heavenly committee of welcome under the presidency of Mi-lo Buddha (the Buddha yet to come). Thang Seng was recognised as a former chief disciple of the Buddha and granted a high rank in Heaven. Monkey was made God of Victorious Strife, and the Pig was created Chief Divine Altar Cleanser. The horse who had carried Thang Seng and the scriptures was turned into a four-clawed dragon and chief of celestial dragons. Now at the beginning of his pilgrimage Thang Seng had fitted on Monkey a helmet which contracted upon his skull when he was wayward or wanton. The agony of the contractions had caused him to refrain from wickedness. When, therefore, he was given his new title Monkey begged Thang Seng to remove the helmet, since he had now become an enlightened one. Thang Seng answered that if Monkey was indeed enlightened, the helmet would have gone of its own accord. And Monkey reached up to feel his head and found that the helmet had disappeared.

The miraculous *chhi-lin*

It seems that in the oldest Chinese tradition the ritualised concept of war was that of justice by ordeal. There was an initial offering of blood, which might perhaps be used to anoint a war-drum; the combat itself was construed as a stylised encounter. On its termination the prisoners were brought to justice at a formal trial in a ceremonial hall and those of double heart were condemned.

Kao-yao, the judge of Shun the last of the Five Emperors and predecessor of Yu, was considered to be the embodiment and exemplar of this justice. The emblem of Kao-yao was the *chhi-lin*, an auspicious creature. Its body was that of a deer, with the tail of an ox, horse's hooves and a single, fleshy horn. The hair on its back was vari-coloured, that on its belly yellow. When it walked it did not crush the grass and it consumed no living creature. It spared the innocent but struck the guilty with its single horn, its action being determined by the findings of the upright judge Kao-yao. In another version, Kao-yao's judgments were executed by a single-horned ram, a story which, it has been suggested,

derives from some type of trial by ordeal involving the offering of such an animal and swearing by its blood.

When the judgments of a prince achieved ideal justice, a *chhi-lin* was born in his court, attracted thither by the beneficent virtue of the prince. The appearance at the imperial court of miraculous beasts was a proof of the favour of Heaven and of the emperor's supreme virtue, for it was only when the cosmic order had achieved a perfect balance that there was a sufficient amount of cosmic force to allow the production of such wonders.

Such an occasion arose during the Ming dynasty, in the reign of the emperor Yung Lo, the third of the Ming line. The whole story is a curious one, for it is involved with the voyages of exploration by the Jewel Ships, under the command of the Three Jewel Eunuch, Cheng Ho, a Muslim from Yunnan, which led the Ming fleet to the coast of Africa in the early fifteenth century. The expeditions were inspired by the appearance in the capital of a giraffe, sent as tribute from Bengal, where it had been imported from Africa. Now the collection of exotic beasts had long been a feature of the imperial capital and during the voyages which the Ming fleet undertook, it had been part of their duties to collect the rare, the strange, the exotic for adding to the imperial treasure. For reasons both complicated and obscure it seems that the professional courtiers, the eunuchs who surrounded the Ming court, contrived that a giraffe should be presented to their ruler. By a curious coincidence the Somali name for giraffe is *girin*, a word which to a Ming Chinese would sound most auspiciously like *chhi-lin*, the name of the emblem of justice, embodiment of princely virtue as expressed in the giving of judgment. Physically, too, the giraffe had points of resemblance to the *chhi-lin*, with its deer-like body, ox-tail, hooves, horn and variegated body with yellow underparts, which did not eat flesh and was of a gentle disposition.

When the giraffe arrived from Bengal there was much excitement at the Ming court, and the Board of Rites expressed a desire to present to the emperor a congratulatory memorial. This was declined by the emperor, who expressed the view that if the ministers exerted themselves for the exercise of good government, then if the world was at peace, there was no hindrance to good rule even without a *chhi-lin*. This was in September 1414. In the following year a second giraffe, procured, it seems most likely, by the court eunuchs, arrived at the court. Once again the emperor declined to receive a memorial of congratulations, but he did proceed in state to the Perfumed Gate to receive a zebra, an oryx and the giraffe in the presence of his prostrated ministers and officials. He attributed the arrival of the auspicious creatures to the abundance of virtue which had accrued to his father the previous emperor and, he added graciously, to the assistance which he had received from his ministers. To this was also to be attributed the constant influx of foreign visitors (all of whom tended, in accordance with a tradition of considerable antiquity, to be treated as coming to China in token of their country's recognition of Chinese suzerainty).

But while the emperor was modestly disclaiming any part in the reappearance of the *chhi-lin*, and indeed inviting his ministers to remonstrate with him over any shortcomings that they might detect in his exercise of the heavenly mandate, others had no doubt of the true reasons for the auspicious manifestation. Painters recorded the miraculous beast and the poet Shen Tu of the Imperial Academy offered an ode explaining that 'when a sage possesses virtue of extreme benevolence so as to illumine the darkest places, a *chhi-lin* appears'. Such an appearance was clear proof that His Majesty's virtue equalled that of Heaven, whose mercy and blessing had been distributed so universally that its harmonious emanations had produced a *chhi-lin* as unending bliss for the state for a myriad, myriad years. Therefore, continued the poet:

I, your servant, joining the multitude, regard respectfully this auspicious

Buddha riding on a dragon. The horse who had carried Thang Seng on his great pilgrimage to the Western Paradise and had faithfully borne back the authentic versions of the Buddha's teachings to China was rewarded by being made into a dragon, and chief of the celestial dragons who guard the mansions of the gods. *c.* seventeenth-eighteenth centuries A.D. Buddhist scroll painting.

Guardian lion of the Sui or early Thang dynasty. *c.* A.D. 600. Some of the most common animal figures in Chinese art fall into the category of miraculous beasts whose presence proved the favour of Heaven. Lions were not native to China, and were treated as fantastic animals, often used to guard tombs. The first examples are Han (second century A.D.). They were much used for four centuries thereafter, lined up in pairs along the Spirit Road to the south of the tomb. Cleveland Museum of Art.

Imperial Dragons and the Flaming Pearl, which represents the sun. The pearl guarded by the dragon in the water represents imperial treasure. Like the Indian Nagarajas, the Dragon Kings kept their treasures in fabulous underwater palaces made of crystal and they fed upon pearls and opals. There were five of them, corresponding to the Five Mountains, and once a year they all rose out of the waters and without wings flew up to Heaven to report to the Supreme Emperor. Kho-ssu silk tapestry panel. Ming dynasty (1368-1644). Seattle Art Museum.

omen and, kneeling a hundred times and knocking my head upon the ground, I present the following hymn of praise:

How glorious is the Sacred Emperor whose literary and military virtues are most excellent,

Who has succeeded to the Precious Throne and has achieved Perfect Order in imitation of the Ancients! Tranquillity prevails throughout the myriad countries and the Three Luminaries follow their due course;

The Hot and the Rainy Seasons occur in due order and each year sees the harvesting of rice and millet;

The people rejoice in their customs without rift or impediment:

In consequence, auspicious manifestations have accurred universally.

A Tsou-yu [vegetarian tiger] has indeed appeared; springs of flavourful water and sweet dew have issued forth.

Miraculous ears have occurred plentifully: the River has run clear.

The occurrence of all the Happinesses is a true token of Heaven's aid,

A true token of Heaven's aid and a proclamation of Heaven's favour.

Now in the twelfth year, in the cyclical position *chia-wu,*

In a corner of the Western Sea, in the stagnant waters of the great marsh,

A *chhi-lin* has in truth been produced, some fifteen feet in height,

Its body that of a deer and with the tail of an ox, with a fleshy horn without bone,

And luminous spots like a red cloud, a purple mist.

Its hooves do not trample upon living creatures and it proceeds with careful tread,

Walking in stately manner and moving in a continuous rhythm.

Its harmonious voice has the sound of a bell or musical tube.

Benevolent is this creature which has appeared but once in all antiquity,

Whose manifestation of divine spirits reaches up to the abode of Heaven.

Ministers and people together vie to be first to gaze upon the joyous spectacle,

As when the Phoenix of Mount Chhi sang in the time of Chou or the River Chart was given to Yu.

The people are united in this year, conforming to the rules of conduct.

Your servant on duty in the Forest of Letters [The Imperial Academy] who presumed to cherish the ambition to record this event,

Has chanted this poem to present a hymn of praise to the Sacred Ruler.

Composed by your servant Shen Tu, *Shih-chiang-hsueh-shih, Feng-hsun-ta-fu* of the Academy of Letters.

In Shen Tu's eyes, the Yung-lo Emperor had achieved the classical ideal: Heaven and Earth were in harmony; the imperial virtue equalled that of Heaven. The appearance of the *chhi-lin* bore witness to the truth of this belief, to the rightness of those who upheld the Confucian tradition, a select group which included the scholars of the Imperial Academy of Letters.

Modern myths

According to Kipling:

> There are nine and sixty ways of
> constructing tribal lays
> And – every – single – one – of –
> them – is – right!

What we have seen so far has consisted almost wholly of the constructions of scholars, men who have been concerned to produce stories which will sustain a specific point of view or illustrate a doctrine, lend support to an hypothesis or justify a course of action. Not all such stories belong to the earliest periods of Chinese history: even today stories are being devised or existing tales modified to advocate what are seen to be socially desirable attitudes.

The prince who could not find a wife

Eberhard recounts a tale collected in Yunnan by Communist folklorists about a prince who sought a bride and was told by an old man that the best flowers bloom in mountain valleys, the best girls grow up among the common people. 'If you search among the people you will be sure to find a suitable partner.' The quest was unsuccessful, however, because, as the old man explained, goats do not befriend wolves, rats do not marry cats; nor can the common people associate with the son of a king. So the prince hid his identity and lived among the people. The story does not say what happened to the king whose only son he had been.

The peasant girl and the princess

Another story in Eberhard's collection from Yunnan, where it is attributed to the partly sinised I, a Thai tribal group, seems to have been strongly influenced by Communist editing. The girl succeeds when the men are helpless; she sacrifices herself for the community; the king's daughter tacitly admits her superiority although the heroine is of lowly origin. Although poor, she is indifferent to the possibility of wealth.

Right. Incense burner in the form of a peacock. The peacock was a symbol of beauty and dignity and, according to the I, a benefactor of mankind, for he advised Sea Girl how to befriend the daughter of the Dragon King and so unlock the waters. Sixteenth-seventeenth century A.D. National Gallery, Prague.

A pair of phoenixes, symbols of happiness and luck and a sign of Heaven's favour. In the time of Chou the Phoenix of Mount Chhi sang as a happy portent. The phoenix, identified with the Empress, was propitious, just as the dragon rain-spirit identified with the Emperor was a beneficent creature. Painting on silk. Possibly Ming dynasty.

In Eberhard's words, 'practically all these traits run counter to Chinese traditional values'.

There was once a man called Chiao who lived with his daughter near Horse Ear Mountain. The girl was called Sea Girl. In a year of great drought, the people were starving and could not live on their produce, so Chiao and his daughter went up into the mountains to cut bamboos for brooms. One day the daughter saw a shining lake whose waters were wholly clear. Any leaf which fell on to its surface was at once carried off by a great wild goose. Sea Girl took her load of bamboos home and the following day went back with an axe to try to cut a passage from the lake to let the waters into the parched lands of her village. She failed in her attempt, but as she sat in despair under a tree deciding what to do next a wild goose appeared and told her that she needed a golden key to open the lake. Before she could ask where one got a golden key, the goose had gone, and she was forced to ask three parrots who were in the wood where she was how she might obtain such a key. They told her to find the third daughter of the Dragon King.

The girl continued her search until she met a peacock, who advised her that the maiden she sought was to be found in the canyons of the southern mountains. As she set out, the peacock flew ahead of her and was able to tell her that the third daughter of the Dragon King liked the songs which the people sang. The girl sang folksongs for three

days and on the third day, as she sang of the flowers which blossomed on the hillside, the third daughter of the Dragon King appeared, although her father had decreed that no member of his kingdom could enter the human world without specific permission. She admired Sea Girl's singing greatly, for she was a great lover of folksongs, and asked her why she sang and whence she came. The girl explained that she was seeking for the golden key in order to release the waters from the lake for the benefit of the parched fields of her village near Horse Ear Mountain.

The king's daughter told her that the key was in the king's treasury under the guard of an eagle who would kill all comers save the king himself. But one day when the king had left the palace, the girl and the princess sang songs in front of the treasury until the eagle woke and, spreading his wings, came to see who was singing. Then the girl slipped past him and into the treasury. The whole was filled with gold and precious jewels, but these the girl disregarded, seeking only to find the key on which her fellow-villagers' survival depended. She found the key by accident, knocking over a wooden box in which it was hidden, and at once hurried back to the third daughter of the Dragon King. The latter stopped singing and the two girls dashed away to the lake; meanwhile, now that the songs had stopped, the eagle fell asleep once more.

Sea Girl used the key to unlock the waters of the lake. There was a great rush of water, and if the Dragon King's daughter had not made her turn off the flow, all the lands of Horse Ear Mountain district would have been disastrously flooded. The girl used straw curtains to stop the threatening flood; these are still there, but the straws have turned to stone. When the Dragon King returned home, he was very angry and banished his daughter, who went to live with Sea Girl and to sing folk-songs with her. The women of the district honour them with communal songs on the twenty-second day of the eleventh month.

Further Reading List

Birch, Cyril. *Chinese myths and fantasies*. Oxford University Press, London, 1962.

Brewitt-Taylor C.H. *Romance of the three Kingdoms* (2 vols.), Shanghai, 1925.

Chang, Kwang-chih. *The archaeology of ancient China*. Yale University Press, New Haven, 1963.

Cheng Te-kun. *Archaeology in China: prehistoric China*. W. Heffer and Sons, Cambridge, 1959.

– *Archaeology in China: Shang China*. W. Heffer and Sons, Cambridge 1961

Duyvendank, J.J.L. *China's discovery of Africa*. Arthur Probsthain, London, 1949.

Eberhard, W. *Folktales of China*. Routledge and Kegan Paul, London, 1965.

– *Lokalkulturen im alten China*. Brill, Leiden, 1943.

– *Typen chinesischer Volksmarchen*. Helsinki, 1937.

Fitzgerald, C. P. *China, a short cultural history*. Cresset Press, London, 1935.

Granet, Marcel. *Danses et légendes de la Chine ancienne*. Félix Alcan, Paris, 1926.

– *Etudes sociologiques sur la Chine*. Presses universitaires de France, Paris, 1953.

Trs. K.E. Innes and M.R. Brailsford. *Chinese civilisation*. Kegan Paul, Trench, Trubner, London, 1930.

– Trs. E.D. Edwards. *Festivals and songs of ancient China*. George Routledge, London, 1932.

Karlgren, B. 'Legends and cults in ancient China'. *Bulletin of the Museum of Far Eastern Antiquities* Vol. 18. Stockholm, 1946.

Maspero, Henri. *Mélanges posthumes sur les religions et l'histoire de la Chine* (3 vols: Les religions chinoises; Le Taoïsme; Etudes historiques). Civilisations du Sud, Paris, 1950.

Doré, Henri. *Recherches sur les superstitions en Chine* (18 vols.), Catholic Mission Press, Shanghai, 1911-38.

Needham, Joseph. *Science and civilisation in China*. Cambridge University Press, Cambridge, 1954 and 1956.

Watson, W. *Early civilisation in China*. Thames and Hudson, London, 1966.

Werner, E.T.C. *Myths and legends of China*. George Harrap, London, 1922.

Acknowledgments

Any writer on Chinese mythology must owe a debt of gratitude to various predecessors. A list of major sources in easily accessible form is given below, but it will be obvious that there are many specific debts both to works listed there and to articles by various scholars who have contributed to the study of Chinese cultural history. In particular the following should be named: Wolfram Eberhard, C. P. Fitzgerald, Marcel Granet and Henri Maspero.

The Publishers gratefully acknowledge the following for permission to reproduce the illustrations indicated:

COLOUR PLATES
Charbonnier-Réalités: 128, 129 top, 129 bott. Giraudon: 73. Paul Hamlyn Library: 26. Michael Holford: frontis., 27, 34 top, 35, 50, 51, 58, 59, 80, 81, 98 right, 99, 103 top, 107, 121, 125. Miniature Gallery, Long Dritton: 34 bott. Seattle Art Museum: 76, 77. John Massey Stewart: 98 left.

BLACK AND WHITE
Arts Council: 28. Bildarchiv Foto Marburg: 31, 66, 93, 108, 110 top, 111 top, 112 top, 115, 118, 122, 131. Britain-China Friendship Assoc.: 88 bott. British Museum: 13, 16, 37, 38, 48, 74 top, 75, 86 bott., 87 top, 119. Camera Press: 97. Cleveland Museum of Art: 65 right, 106 top, 133, 138. Cowderoy and Moss, Ltd.: 64. Fine Art Engravers, Ltd.: 53. Werner Forman: 20, 30, 104, 112 bott., 114 bott., 135. Raymond Fortt: half title. John R. Freeman: 49. Freer Gallery, Washington, D.C.: 29. Giraudon: 43, 63, 113. Paul Hamlyn Library: 17 top, 21, 23, 25, 54, 55, 62, 83 right, 86 top, 89, 114 top, 130, 134. Michael Holford: 67, 92, 95, 105, 117. Mansell Collection: 72. Metropolitan Museum of Art, New York: 41, 84 right, 85, 111 bott., 116. Minneapolis Institute of Arts: 14, 17 bott., 18, 42, 82 left. Musée Cernuschi: 32 bott., 68 left. Musée Guimet: 22, 36. Museum of Far Eastern Antiquities, Stockholm: 12. Museum of Fine Arts, Boston: 44-45. National Gallery, Prague: 74 bott. National Palace Museum, Taiwan: 39, 56 top, 57, 68-69, 79, 84 left. Osaka Municipal Museum of Fine Arts: 61. Rietbergmuseum, Zurich: 56 bott. Seattle Art Museum: 10, 24, 33, 52, 82, 101, 132. Sperryn's Ltd.: 91, 123. University of Hong Kong: 78, 87 bott., 88 top, 90. Franco Vanotti: 32 top. Victoria and Albert Museum: 65 left, 70, 71, 96, 106 bott., 109, 110 bott., 120, 127. William Rockhill Nelson Gallery of Art, Kansas City: 19, 47 top and bott., 46 top and bott.

Index